T0339447

Dear School Leader

Dear school leader, you have a big impact on your teachers and students! In this follow-up to the bestselling *Dear Teacher*, motivational speaker Dr. Brad Johnson provides 50 inspiring quotes for leaders, along with stories and practical takeaways, to thank you for all that you do and to help you thrive in your role.

Dr. Brad Johnson covers topics such as focusing on your assets instead of your agenda; remembering your purpose; embracing failure; overcoming imposter syndrome and decision fatigue; celebrating the small things; becoming a world class you; and more!

The book is perfect to gift to the principals and other administrators in your life, or for your own nightly reading as you reflect on the day. The uplifting advice will help you focus on your purpose in this profession – and will help you remember that even when you're having a bad day, you're making a positive difference!

Brad Johnson (@DrBradJohnson) has nearly 30 years of experience as a teacher and administrator at the K-12 and collegiate level. He is author of several books and one of the most inspirational and affirmational speakers in education. Dr. Johnson has recently been recognized as a Top 30 Global Guru in Education.

Dear School Leader

50 Motivational Quotes and Anecdotes that Affirm Your Purpose and Your Impact

Brad Johnson

Routledge
Taylor & Francis Group

NEW YORK AND LONDON

Designed cover image: © Getty Images

First published 2024
by Routledge
605 Third Avenue, New York, NY 10158

and by Routledge
4 Park Square, Milton Park, Abingdon, Oxon, OX14 4RN

Routledge is an imprint of the Taylor & Francis Group, an informa business

Library of Congress Cataloging-in-Publication Data
Names: Johnson, Brad, 1969– author.
Title: Dear school leader : 50 motivational quotes and anecdotes that affirm your purpose and your impact / Brad Johnson.
Description: New York : Routledge, 2023.
Identifiers: LCCN 2022060770 | ISBN 9781032311340 (hbk) | ISBN 9781032288239 (pbk) | ISBN 9781003308218 (ebk)
Subjects: LCSH: School principals—United States. | Teachers—United States. | Educational leadership—Psychological aspects. | School management and organization—United States.
Classification: LCC LB2831.92 .J64 2023 | DDC 371.2/012—dc23/eng/20230301
LC record available at https://lccn.loc.gov/2022060770

ISBN: 978-1-032-31134-0 (hbk)
ISBN: 978-1-032-28823-9 (pbk)
ISBN: 978-1-003-30821-8 (ebk)

DOI: 10.4324/9781003308218

Typeset in Palatino
by Apex CoVantage, LLC

Contents

Preface

Dear School Leader,

School administrators have a tough and sometimes lonely job. I have often said school leaders, especially principals, have one of the toughest jobs trying to balance mandates and the expectations for the district while supporting and encouraging their staff. And this doesn't include supporting and working with parents and students. You have tons of responsibility, with little authority or autonomy to really run a school exactly how you would like to run it. It can be a downright exhausting job! I jokingly share with administrators that you may have the only job where someone is always mad at you simply because of your position.

So, let me say Thank You! Thank you for all you do for your staff, students, and school community. Thank you for the countless hours you spend in school, after school, and interacting with the board and the community outside of school time as well. It almost seems like you are on call 24/7. But you do it for the benefit of the students, teachers, and the community.

Never underestimate the difference you are making. I believe teachers and staff are the difference makers for the students. But you are the difference maker for the difference makers! While it takes everyone to create a dynamic school culture, never forget you are the thermostat for that culture. Yes, it is a lot of work, responsibility, and often very little appreciation for your role, but you are impacting lives every day – and some lives forever.

I wrote this book to be an encouragement to you, inspiration for you, and to thank you for all you do for your teachers and staff every day!

Meet the Author

Dr. Brad Johnson is one of the most dynamic and engaging speakers in the fields of education and leadership. He has nearly 30 years of experience in the trenches as a teacher and administrator. Dr. Johnson is transforming how teachers lead in the classroom and how administrators lead in the school. He is a servant leader who shares his vast experiences and expertise to help other educators maximize their potential. He is author of many books including *Dear Teacher* (with Hal Bowman), *Principal Bootcamp*, *Putting Teachers First*, and *Learning on Your Feet*. He has travelled the globe speaking and training teachers and educational leaders.

1

You Don't Have to Be Perfect to Be Great!

Did you know the pursuit of perfection is the greatest hindrance to greatness? Perfection is the unrealistic and unnecessary pressure put on oneself to be something you are not and cannot be.

I think as educational leaders, you often feel the pressure to be perfect because there are such unrealistic expectations actually put on you. Whether it is the expectation of the district to turn around a low performing school in months, or unrealistic expectations from parents, or even teachers, you may feel like you have to be perfect at all times.

And maybe even worse is the pressure administrators often place on themselves to be able to do it all, to always be all in, to be perfect. Thinking you must be perfect will usually do one of two things. First of all, it will be so overwhelming that it will paralyze someone from trying new things or taking risks. You second guess your decisions and everything you do, because anything less than perfect would be a failure and thus you think you are a failure. Secondly, you will never feel like you do enough to be perfect. You can't be perfect if you don't work 12 hours a day, weekends, holidays, and summer. You have created a situation where you have no off switch, and this is why many administrators burn out.

DOI: 10.4324/9781003308218-1

Some of us have been conditioned to think that "great" isn't as good as "perfect," and that perfection is actually attainable. Yet, in contrast, mere high achievers tend to do better than their perfectionistic counterparts because they are generally less stressed and are satisfied with a job well done. They don't pick it apart and try to zero in on what could have been better.

I have a friend who was a major league baseball player. I won't reveal his name since I share this story when I speak to school districts. But I remember him telling me once that when he was drafted, his goal wasn't to be the best baseball player ever, to win a world series or Cy Young Award, or even to get into the Hall of Fame. His goal was to give up 200 home runs! Now that may sound like a crazy goal, but when you think about it, it is a good goal. He knew that to give up that many home runs, it would take a long time, and that meant longevity. In sports, longevity means you are successful, because if you aren't very good, then you won't be around long. The average career of a pro athlete is around three years. But imagine if he thought he had to be perfect to be great or even to be successful? Imagine what would have happened when he gave up his first home run? It could have crushed his confidence and made him feel defeated immediately. But instead, when he gave up that first home run, he thought alright! Just 199 to go. By the way, he did achieve all of the accolades I mentioned in the beginning, but it was because he removed the pressure of being perfect and was free to become great! What if you knew you had to fail 20 times before you fulfilled your dreams? What about 200 times? **What if we no longer see failure as the end but as just a step toward greatness?**

I remember sharing that story at a district workshop, and a lady came up to me afterwards and said, "I can't wait to go home and figure out what my 200 home runs are!"

What a great perspective for all of us to take. I have said before that I have had many doors closed that I really wanted open, but I wouldn't be where I am today if I had been allowed to pass through them. So don't get paralyzed or burned out by trying to be perfect. Rather seek to bring your best! And remember that you don't have to be perfect to be great!

2

Bring Your Assets, Not Your Agenda

I believe one of the most telling signs of a servant leader is that they are other focused. In my book *Principal Bootcamp*, I use the term selfless leader. This means to be more focused on helping those you lead improve their situation, than on improving your own situation. There is nothing inherently wrong with having high aspirations and wanting to move to the next level, but never let that be your focus. If that is your focus, then you will always be more worried about yourself than about those you lead.

I remember interviewing Mike Abrashoff a few years ago. He was the captain of the *USS Benfold*. He shared the time when he was to take over as commander of the ship. His first experience was the reception aboard the ship to bid the former captain farewell. The crew seemed glad and relieved that the former captain was leaving. It turns out that the former captain was a very intelligent man, but he made the crew feel inferior and was condescending to them, which negatively affected the culture of the ship. The ship's performance was ranked last in the fleet, and the crew didn't feel safe should they be called into action.

Abrashoff recalled (as quoted in Johnson, 2016)[1], "As I watched the ceremony that day and the reaction of the crew, I wondered to myself how the crew would react when I leave the ship after my tenure as captain?" He said this put things into

DOI: 10.4324/9781003308218-2

perspective quickly for him. He knew his goal was to focus on improving the morale of the crew. He said:

> At this point in my career, other than sinking the ship, I knew I was set as far as retirement and even advancing in rank, so my goal wasn't to use the appointment to simply advance. Instead, I wanted to make a real difference in the crew of this ship.

Over the course of his tenure as captain, Abrashoff implemented many strategies which helped build a positive culture. For instance, he created an environment where the crew felt safe to take risks and take ownership in the crew's success. As Abrashoff replied, "I took responsibility for the actions of the crew, so they knew I had their back, even if they failed." Captain Abrashoff would also publicly praise the crew when they did good work – in fact, the crew affectionately named him "Mega Mike" because he would constantly praise his crew, which improved morale.

He didn't see them just as a crew, but he got to know them personally and found out their interests and their strengths, so he could best utilize their talents aboard the ship. Over the course of approximately two years, Abrashoff so profoundly changed the culture of the USS Benfold that it went from being a lower performing ship in the Navy to the best ship in the fleet.

Imagine if more leaders focused on using their strengths and talents to help those they lead improve their lives and become leaders. Then again, what if we all lived our lives in such a manner. **Imagine if we did things for others just because**. No agenda, no hidden motive, but just selfless acts that help others.

I remember a comedian John Pinette who would walk the streets in cities where he performed, and he would carry a pocket of five dollar bills to hand out to people in need. He said he was so fortunate in life that he just wanted to give back even if it was just a little to help someone else. No agenda, no cameras filming it, but just a selfless act. So, as you go through your day, don't just think "what can I do to improve my situation," but "what can I do to help make someone's day a little better too."

Note

1   Johnson, B. (2016). *Principal bootcamp: Accelerated strategies to influence and lead from day one.* Routledge.

3

Your Purpose Is Greater than Your Struggle

The past few years have been a real struggle for educators. Mandates, adjustments, closures, mixed delivery of instruction, and the list goes on. In fact, things have been so crazy that it is easy to focus on the struggles, and if you're not careful, it's easy to feel discouraged and even defeated. But the mission, the work that you do is so very important.

Over the past three years, we've all had days where we don't feel successful, or we feel like we have failed, but that doesn't mean we are failures. Whether you have been struggling for a day, week, or month, remember your mission, your purpose.

In fact, I am reminded of the time when Mother Teresa had a senator from the US visit her in Calcutta and her facility called the House of the Dying. There, sick children are cared for in their last days, and the poor line up by the hundreds to receive medical attention. The senator watched Mother Teresa minister to these people and was overcome by the magnitude of the suffering she and her co-workers faced daily. "How can you bear the load without being crushed beneath it?" the Senator asked. Mother Teresa replied, "My dear Senator, I am not called to be successful; I am called to be faithful."

As an administrator, you may feel like you are being crushed under the weight of all the expectations related to the pandemic,

DOI: 10.4324/9781003308218-3

learning, loss, and everything else thrown at you. With the pressures and expectations on you, you may feel like you aren't successful most days, but remember it's not about success so much as being faithful to your purpose. **Leaders, you are exactly who your staff needs right now.** So remember that as you enter the school building today.

I have shared this quote, "Your purpose is greater than your struggles" on social media and love when educators take time to reply that it was timely or needed. For example:

> "Oh my, I needed this. THANK you for this reminder that my struggle doesn't mean I'm useless to all in everything. I am only one, but I am someone; I can't do everything, but I can do something."

In these unprecedented times, holding fast to our purpose may be all that keeps us afloat. It is our raft in the "white water" of change.

So don't get discouraged by your struggles – although they are real – but hold fast to your purpose because it may be all that is keeping you (and those you lead) afloat. Know that you are a difference maker because your purpose is greater than your struggle.

4

Sometimes You Have to Scoop the Poop

Poop scooping may not sound very motivational, but I assure you it can be. I use this term when I am specifically talking about servant leadership.

Servant leadership seems to be a common narrative in education these days. The theoretical framework was developed in the '60s and '70s by Robert Greenleaf. It almost seems cliché for leaders to think of themselves as servant leaders today, but do they walk the walk?

Servant leaders exhibit traits such as empathy, listening, and awareness, but there are also traits like caring and humility. So, I wonder how many are truly willing to serve those they lead.

If you are a leader and you don't have a pooper scooper, then you aren't prepared to be a servant leader. You know the kind used to scoop out a cat litter box or if you are out walking a dog. I think one of the most important traits of a servant leader is the willingness to jump in when IT hits the fan (or hits the floor!) and help out.

A few months ago, I was at Atlanta's Hartsfield-Jackson airport waiting to fly out to a speaking engagement. Hartsfield-Jackson was busy as usual, since it is the busiest airport in the world. As I sat there observing people, as I often do, I noticed a disabled veteran walking through the terminal with his service dog. The dog was a big, beautiful German Shepherd. It must

DOI: 10.4324/9781003308218-4

have been a long flight and the dog must have eaten well, because the dog pooped on the floor in the middle of the terminal. And it was a lot of poop, and I understood the meaning of "when it hits the fan," or in this case when it hits the floor! I was thinking finally a little excitement to get my day started! My first instinct was to rush right over, but I decided to just observe for a minute and see what happened. I mean after all, these people were flying off to business meetings where they talk about being servant leaders, right? So, I figured several would jump into action to help the man out. Well, I was wrong! Not one person offered to help scoop the poop! Not one person in the busiest airport in the world. One person walking by offered him some paper towels but didn't offer to help him. I guess that was a semi-servant leader! I couldn't take it anymore and grabbed my luggage and walked over to help him. I asked if I could have the paper towels and asked if someone could grab more out of the restroom, because like I said the dog had apparently eaten a Thanksgiving dinner!

So, I knelt down and started literally scooping the poop. I wish I had a scooper at that moment, but the paper towels had to do. He started to kneel down and help and I said no sir, I am happy to do this. As I picked up poop, I asked him about his dog. Her name was Ginger and he said she had been with him for eight years and this is the first time anything like this had ever happened. I thought about saying well it happens, but I said we all have bad days. Ginger was laying there so sweet, and so I was able to pet her on head as I waited for my paper towels. I told you it was a lot of poop. Finally, it was all up and I thanked him for his service and told him to go take care of his sweet dog.

I don't tell this story to brag on myself. **But I think we have more people talking about serving than actually doing the serving. What if we saw serving as a privilege rather than an obligation?** Because, I have to admit I left there more inspired and full of joy than I ever imagined I could. Just because I didn't miss an opportunity to serve.

This reminds me of a tweet I sent out the other day that said, "Servant leaders don't just serve, support, and encourage those they lead, but they also protect, defend, and take care of them." It is not a weak endeavor. It is said that servant leadership provides as much fulfillment for the leader as for those they lead. So, be willing to get out your pooper scooper when it hits the fan or the floor. Because serving others doesn't just help them, but it can bring inspiration and joy to you as well.

5

Choose Your Attitude Each Morning

As educators, we may feel like we have very little control over our lives, especially our work lives. But there are some things we can control, like our attitude. I truly believe that our day is going to be bad or great based largely in part on how we wake up. It's like the adage that we are what we eat – well we are what we think, too! In fact, there is a Proverb which basically says as a person thinks, so they are.

Steve Harvey shared about a rough time in his life on his website (https://steveharvey.com/wake-up-right-steve-harvey-stories/). Harvey said, "I was going through a rough period in my life. I had just been laid off and was on unemployment. At the time I signed up for Amway and my sponsor would call me at 5:30AM every morning. I would answer with a mumble, and he would say 'Steve, this is John Walker, how you doing man? How you feeling? It's going to be a great day!' Well, I had a bad attitude when he called, because I was laid off and couldn't see my future and it was 5:30AM! He called me 37 straight days with the same positive attitude. On the 38th day he called and said 'I'm disappointed in you, when are you going to change your attitude? You wake up with a bad attitude, which pretty much explains why you're having a lot of bad days. I hate that about you, because you have so much potential.'"

DOI: 10.4324/9781003308218-5

When he hung up, Steve said that really hit him hard. Someone thinking he is something and yet he has been acting like that? So, the next morning when John called, Stave said, "Hey John! It's Steve Harvey, how you doing man? It's going to be a great day!" And he has been waking up that way ever since!

And maybe you have been through a lot. Maybe you have let negativity slide into your daily attitude. And did you know that when you have a negative attitude, you attract negativity?

- ◆ Poor performance
- ◆ Unwilling to collaborate
- ◆ Reduced energy levels
- ◆ Depressed feelings
- ◆ Low morale

But when you wake up with a positive attitude, you find that it positively affects your day with:

- ◆ Increased productivity
- ◆ Greater probability of collaboration and teamwork
- ◆ Improved morale
- ◆ Ability to overcome adversity
- ◆ Increased sense of well-being

So, as you start today, focus on the positives in your life. **Set the tone for the day by focusing on a positive attitude.** A positive attitude will not only help you be amazing today, but just like John Walker, your attitude may just help someone else make their day amazing too!

6

Don't Make Any
More Excuses!

Psychologists place excuse-making in what is called a "self-handicapping" category – that is, it's a behavior we express that hurts our own performance and motivation. It serves as a distraction of sorts that prevents us from achieving the task or goal, but it stems from a deeper, unconscious desire to protect ourselves against anxiety and shame. And the more anxious or ashamed we are likely to feel, the more likely we are to build barriers that impede our chances of attaining a goal.

I remember working with a teacher who seemed to be late every day. No, the teacher wasn't me, but it was a male teacher. What was most irritating is that he always had an excuse for being late. For instance, traffic was bad, there was an accident, he was running low on gas, and the list goes on and on and on. In fact, he seemed to think that as long as he had a good excuse, that it was okay to be continually late. He never did admit that he was late because he overslept, or just didn't leave in time or didn't want to stop and get gas the night before so that he could get to school on time.

You see, excuses aim to shift the focus from issues pertaining to our sense of self to issues that are relatively less central or out of our control. And just like this teacher, we feel like if it is a good excuse, then everything is okay.

DOI: 10.4324/9781003308218-6

However, even the best excuses are still just excuses! They give us permission to not be our best, or they keep us from accomplishing our goals. For example, how often do you put off things like going back to school, trying for a new position, or pursuing a passion by coming up with as many excuses as possible for not doing them or at least putting them off until "one day"?

And the sad part is that if we come up with good enough excuses, then we feel better about not pursuing those goals or passions. But what if you were to tell yourself, "No more excuses!" I often use the example of exercising when I talk about no more excuses, because I think we can all relate to it. I know many adults who tell me they just don't have time to exercise, but these same people will watch an hour or two hours of television every night. In fact, did you know the average adult watches over five hours of television each day? Now I know that's not the average teacher, but you have to learn to find time for what is important to you.

So, make up your mind that you are not going to make any more excuses, but you are going to pursue the goals and interests that you have been putting off for months or even years. **Make a plan, set goals, and then accept no more excuses.** For instance, it may take a year or two to complete a doctorate, write a book, or move to the next level in leadership, but the time is going to pass either way, so why not get started on your long-awaited goals now? It doesn't matter if you don't achieve all of those goals, and it certainly doesn't matter what others think about them or you. I don't want to sound overly dramatic, but we really do only get one chance at life, and it is a limited time, so stop letting fear, anxiety, and excuses keep you from achieving your goals!

7

Failure Is a Comma, Not a Period

I am not sure where this thought originated, but it has been a motto I have used throughout life. I remember sharing this once and a teacher said, "I love punctuation inspiration!" Apparently, she was an English teacher, so I am glad I got the punctuation right.

But failure is part of the human experience. It is not a matter of if you will ever fail, but when. And it is okay that you failed. If it were easy, you wouldn't have failed. Your failure was likely the result of you doing something difficult, something new and challenging. So, in reality, be proud that you even attempted whatever led to the failure.

Unfortunately, in society, we have made failure a four-letter word to avoid at all cost. We associate failure with being a failure. You may be struggling right now in your own life. You may feel like you are failing your students, or failing your staff, or failing to keep a healthy balance between work and school. **Just know that whenever you feel like you're failing, it doesn't mean you *are* a failure, and it doesn't mean that it is permanent.**

The problem isn't failure, but how we respond to it. It seems to be human nature that we focus on what we don't do well rather than what we do well. And this doesn't mean we should take failure lightly. I think it's important to always try our best to

DOI: 10.4324/9781003308218-7

succeed, but there are times when we learn as much from failure as we do from success.

In the sports world, especially for youth sports, there's a saying that there is no winning or losing, just winning and learning. I think this is important for us to remember as adults and to teach our students as well. The focus shouldn't be just about the outcome but about growing and learning from the process.

1. Reflect on your failure.
2. But don't dwell on it.
3. Remember failing is learning.
4. Surround yourself with supportive people.

And remember many successful people have failed miserably, so just realize you are in good company with very famous people who failed famously!

Abraham Lincoln

Oprah

Colonel Sanders

Finally, I have my own personal take on failure. Failure is a good thing because it makes us uncomfortable. Think about it, if you never really pushed yourself, or failed, then you would never stretch your limits or grow. You would never reach your full potential.

A great illustration is working out. If you go through the motions every day using the same weights or only weights you can easily handle, then you are not going to get maximum results. In fact, you will see little growth at all. But, if you want growth and success, then you have to push the limits – to go to failure, if you will – to see the best results. It is part of the process of success, not an obstacle to it.

Remember failure is just a comma, so when you feel like you have failed, pause and take a breath! Reflect, make adjustments, and then continue to move forward. Failure is not fatal or final. It is just an uncomfortable, but necessary part of the process to success.

8

Celebrate All Successes

Celebrations actually boost our well-being. This is true for major milestones and daily wins alike. One of the main reasons celebrating is so important is because it reflects an overall attitude of gratitude and enjoying what we have now in the moment, instead of focusing on what we don't have or on what we want in the future.

Whether you work with students or even adults, never take anything for granted. It's important to celebrate small successes. Think of the student who finally got his first A on an exam. Or think of the teacher who does a special project, or even gets an advanced degree. In the big picture of life, these may not seem like much, but in the moment, they are huge!

After all, educators tend to speak the language of affirmation (emotional support and encouragement) to their students, so make sure they get to be celebrated themselves!

We also need to celebrate often and not just at designated times. Often, we wait until the end of the semester or year or some other "big event" to celebrate successes, such as academic awards. Well, over time, the small wins will be forgotten and seem unimportant. Recognizing these small wins is as much about being timely as anything else. Living in the moment keeps us inspired and moving forward. It can be hard to build momentum, so start with small wins, small moments, and let them build.

DOI: 10.4324/9781003308218-8

The best way to have a successful year is to secure small wins, because small wins often make a huge difference. These small wins make work more meaningful and inspire us to continue forward. **Celebrate the small successes because they transform moments into the momentum for even greater things.** Sometimes I think we forget the importance of living in the moment and celebrating the small wins. Don't overlook the importance of celebrating.

I have a good friend whom I used to workout with at the gym, and he had a skiing accident a couple of months ago. Now, this was a guy who worked out daily, played sports, and loved the outdoors. Unfortunately, in the accident he was paralyzed from the chest down. So, for the last couple of months, he has been in rehab at the Shepherd Center, which is one of the top spinal cord injury facilities in the world. But what has impressed me most is not the facilities, which are amazing, or even the skills of the doctors, which are also amazing. It is how they treat their patients and celebrate every improvement they make.

What is also special is that even though everyone there is going through a life changing process for themselves, they still cheer each other on and celebrate everyone's successes. In fact, one of them graduated the other day and went home. They have something called The Dory Award that is given by a person leaving the program to a peer they saw fighting for their new life to be the best possible. Someone who clearly wants to get better and never gives up. This award was handed to him by his peer. He was so excited and overwhelmed by this. He now gets to watch new peers coming in and to pick one who stands out to him for when it's time for him to leave. And yes, they get a stuffed Dory fish, who was known for her optimism and phrase "just keep swimming" in the movie *Finding Nemo*.

So, let's take that optimism into this week. Let's live in the moment. Let's celebrate the small wins, the small victories, because for some they may actually be big wins. And never forget that even the small moments can build momentum into bigger wins in school and in life!

9

Add to the Calm, Not to the Chaos

Whether you are in the classroom or the boardroom, a trait of an effective leader is to be a thermostat and not a thermometer. A thermometer measures the temperature or reflects the environment that it is in, while a thermostat sets the temperature or controls the environment. Do you control your working environment, or do you let it control you? In other words, do you influence your environment or are you influenced by it?

When you are a thermometer, you may become negative if you are around negativity, or you may add to the chaos in the middle of chaos. When you are a thermostat, you influence the environment of your school. This means you have to be careful not to influence it in a negative manner such as by adding negativity or chaos to the climate. You should be creating a climate of trust, collaboration, and teamwork by adding encouragement, support, and praise.

If you want to know how effective you are as a thermostat, then ask yourself if people are more positive and focused when you are around, or if you make the climate less effective. Your attitude can even affect the climate. **Being a thermostat is not an easy task, but it is critical to creating a positive working environment.** I think one of the best reminders related to the importance of being the thermostat is to make sure you are making

DOI: 10.4324/9781003308218-9

things better and not worse, or as I like to say, adding to the calm, not to the chaos.

I remember a couple of years ago when I was flying to Malaysia to speak at teaching centers throughout the country. We were about ten hours into the flight, somewhere down the coast of Russia toward Japan, when we hit some major turbulence. It was the middle of the night, but I was awake, because I can't sleep on airplanes. I guess I feel like I need to be awake in case the pilots need me to help fly the plane or something. After a few bumps and quick drops, the pilot came over the speaker and requested the flight attendants to take a seat and buckle up immediately. You could see the fear on the flight attendants' faces as they rushed to their seats. But what was interesting is that you couldn't hear the fear in the pilot's voice.

He continued to talk calmly to us as the plane was tossed around like a salad 30,000 feet in the air. The pilot talked us through what seemed like hours but was probably more like ten minutes. And in those few minutes, I thought that it might be the end. After the plane settled and we cheered, I asked the flight attendant to let the pilot know we appreciated his calmness under pressure. He created a climate of calmness in what could have been a chaotic situation.

You are the pilot of the plane, the thermostat of the school, or whatever analogy you want to use, but you are the one everyone looks to in a crisis. So take a deep breath, focus on the issues, and make good decisions that will add to the calm and not to the chaos.

10

Be a World Class You!

I don't think I have ever given a speech where I didn't include this concept. I am by nature a maximizer influencer, which means that my main strength is to help people recognize their own strengths and maximize them! That's why I rarely talk about weaknesses or make them a major focus. That's mainly because improving them will do little to help you be successful, but developing your talents or strengths will help you be exponentially more successful.

In fact, developing your talents and passions is the only way you can become your world class self! Administrators, especially new ones, may feel like they have to be just like other leaders. But you don't need to be a copy of anyone; you simply need to build on your strengths to be your best self.

They say there are two important days in your life: the day you were born and the day you realize why you were born. We were all born with purpose. Our purpose is typically found when we identify and develop our talents and our passions. In fact, there is not much more inspiring than identifying and living out your purpose. When leaders identify their strengths and passions and utilize them in the school and school community, they can have a profound impact on the success of those they lead!

The problem is that in our culture, we are always focused on our weaknesses. Commercials are geared toward what we are missing or what we need to be better. Even in education, we often see so much emphasis placed on correcting weaknesses

DOI: 10.4324/9781003308218-10

rather than on developing strengths. And the harder something is to do, then the more valued we think it must be, because it took hard work and rigor to make it better! And so, we rarely value our strengths and talents because they do come easier for us. Which is ironic because our talents and strengths are what set us apart, what make us stand out.

I remember one of the last conversations I had with my dad before he passed away several years ago. He said, "Son, follow your path. Don't worry what others say you should do or what path you think is expected of you, but follow your path. Walk in your purpose." And let me tell you, I am so glad that I have. I loved teaching and I loved being an administrator, but they were just steps to get me to my purpose which I am living out daily.

The formula is simply: Strengths + Passions = Purpose.

What are your strengths, or things you do well? What are your passions or things that stir your emotions? When you can combine strengths and passions, they can help you identify your purpose. Many educators feel that it is not just a job but a calling or purpose. So, focus on developing your best self, develop your talents, and become a world class you! You will be more inspired and invigorated in your teaching, and you just may help inspire others to be their best selves too!

11

Overcome Imposter Syndrome

Imposter syndrome can be defined as doubting your abilities and feeling like a fraud. It shows up in someone who finds it difficult to accept their accomplishments. Many will even question whether they're deserving of an accolade. You experience a persistent fear that you're going to be "found out" or discovered as a fraud, in spite of successes. For instance, as an administrator, you may be afraid your staff may not think you are up to the job. And even when you achieve success, you attribute it to luck or describe it as a fluke. You might feel relief or even distress in place of happiness and pride. You look for validation from authority figures – such as a boss or family member – and give them the power to dictate whether you are successful or not. It disproportionately affects high-achieving people, which may be why it seems to be more common than you think among educators.

Now if you are new to a role, such as a first year AP or even a principal, it is perfectly acceptable to have self-doubts, because you are a novice in your new role or to a new school. In fact, if you didn't have any self-doubts, you might be narcissistic. And having those doubts will serve you well in continuing to grow and learn to become an expert in your new role. But even then, it shouldn't be a persistent feeling of inadequacy or high anxiety.

The first thing that helps change this perception is your self-talk. So, what is your recorder playing? Every time you have a negative thought about your abilities or wonder if you're qualified for a job, pause and ask yourself: Is the thought actually (truly)

DOI: 10.4324/9781003308218-11

accurate? Is this emotional experience real, or am I responding based on other outside variables? Do these thoughts help or hinder me? We can overcome a lot of self-doubt and anxiety by changing how we talk to ourselves. Remind yourself you are a highly educated, highly trained professional. **You have talents and abilities that make you competent. Repeat that to yourself often!**

- ◆ **Talk it out.** Whether it's a mentor, friend, or colleague, talk to someone else about how you're feeling. Getting an outside perspective can shake irrational beliefs and ground you in reality. This can be effective because ironically others can often see our talents and strengths when we can't see them ourselves. So listen to them and believe them when they tell you how competent and amazing you are!
- ◆ **Embrace even small successes.** If you have imposter syndrome, it can be tempting to invalidate even the smallest win. Resist that urge by listing every success and allowing them to resonate emotionally. Over time, this practice will give you a realistic picture of your accomplishments and help affirm your self-worth.

So as you begin this week, change your mindset to build your confidence. Practice self-love, take credit for your achievements, improve your self-talk, and learn to appreciate what you have right now, without worrying about what's going to happen tomorrow – or what happened yesterday. Realize just how much you have accomplished, and let that be the catalyst to achieve even greater things!

12

It's Okay to Have a Bad Day!

I heard a comedian say it's important to be as positive as possible, but sometimes you just have a bad day. Sometimes you just want to go to Walmart and smack the smile off the greeter. While we would never do such a thing, we can relate to the sentiment because education, regardless of your role, is not an easy job. But as an administrator, you are often expected to be all smiles and positive regardless of what is going on in your life. Which, let's be honest, is really a lot of pressure!

We can relate to bad days and occasionally a bad week. I think the problem with many educators is that we work so hard and have a tendency to expect perfection from ourselves and to expect that we always have to give our students or staff our very best. But there are times when the cup is almost empty, or maybe the cup even has a crack. It is just part of being a human. When those days happen, and they will, just realize that sometimes simply surviving is a victory!

I think the key to limiting these days is to do a self-health check. Are you getting enough sleep, are you eating properly, and are you taking care of yourself? If these are the issues, then you definitely have control over those areas and can make changes. If it is work related, then look for ways to lighten your load for a day or two and focus on taking care of yourself. **The world won't end if everything isn't done at the end of the day.**

DOI: 10.4324/9781003308218-12

When you're having a bad day, it can feel like things will never get better. However, the fact is that tomorrow is a new day and a new opportunity to improve things.

Here are a few keys to remember, even in the midst of a bad day or even week:

- ♦ There is a lesson in every struggle.
- ♦ Hard times help you appreciate the good.
- ♦ It is okay to ask for help.
- ♦ It is okay to cry.

Just remember that bad days are temporary. Feel what you need to feel, and then allow yourself to move on to better days. I would say have the memory of a goldfish, because I have always heard a goldfish only has a three- or four-second memory. But I actually researched it and found out that isn't really the case. I think someone probably came up with that stat because we keep goldfish in tiny little bowls, so we hope they have short memories because life has to be really boring in that little bowl. So whether or not a goldfish actually has a four-second memory, try to have one yourself on those bad days. Because there is not much worse than a bad day, except replaying it over and over in your mind!

And remember what I think is one of the best old adages there is, "and this too shall pass." Because even when you have a bad day or are going through a tough situation, just remember that it too will pass. That will give you hope for a better day tomorrow!

13

Alleviate the Decision Fatigue

In education, we often joke there is tired, and then there is teacher tired. I don't think many people understand this truth, unless you have survived the first week or weeks of school. For the first few years of teaching, I remember going home after school and falling asleep for hours. Sometimes bedtime was before sunset.

But this rings true for educational leaders as well. One of the reasons that administrators feel so worn out is because of decision fatigue. Educators make more minute-by-minute decisions than brain surgeons, and that's extremely tiring. And the brain surgeon doesn't have to deal with a school full of students.

Every choice you make throughout the day taxes your mind and reduces your ability to make good decisions later in the day. Not to mention that you are trying to keep a staff of 100 or more focused on the same goals and vision. That's why there are days when you go home and you are so exhausted that you don't feel like doing anything around the house, except taking a nap on the sofa. So how can you help alleviate some of this decision fatigue?

It's different from ordinary physical fatigue – you're not consciously aware of being tired – but you're low on mental energy. **The more choices you make throughout the day, the harder each one becomes for your brain.** Eventually it looks for shortcuts, usually in either of two very different ways. One shortcut is to become reckless: to act impulsively instead of expending the energy to first think through the consequences. (Sure, tweet that photo! Or reply to that negative comment, what could go

DOI: 10.4324/9781003308218-13

wrong?) The other shortcut is the ultimate energy saver: do nothing. Instead of agonizing over decisions, avoid any choice. Ducking a decision often creates bigger problems in the long run, but for the moment, it eases the mental strain.

Create routines and become organized so you have fewer decisions to make throughout the day. Make sure you are getting adequate sleep. Make healthier food choices, and try to include exercise as much as possible. Try to limit decisions, especially important ones, later in the day when a bad choice is more likely. This means whether they involve personal or professional decisions, make them earlier in the day when you can focus better. Have meetings earlier in the day or work on harder tasks earlier in the day if possible. Take time out during the day to visit classrooms and just enjoy engaging with teachers and students. Finally, on days you feel the need, fall asleep on the sofa when you get home. Trust me, none of us will judge you, and it may just be the best decision you make all day!

14

Change What Your Recorder Is Playing

Did you know most of our conversations throughout the day are with ourselves? So the question I have for you is, what are you telling yourself?

Our self-talk or inner recording can affect our effectiveness as a leader and even affect our personal lives. Too often our self-talk may be negative. What happens after you've done something embarrassing? Does your inner voice say, "Well that was dumb"? What if you haven't even done anything wrong, but your self-talk is just as critical? Are you more likely to criticize yourself or to build yourself up?

Negative self-talk tends to fall into one of four categories:

1. **Personalizing** – Meaning you blame yourself when things go wrong
2. **Polarizing** – Meaning you see things only as good or bad, no gray areas or room for middle ground
3. **Magnifying** – Meaning you only focus on the bad or negative in every scenario and dismiss anything good or positive
4. **Catastrophizing** – Meaning you always expect the worst

Understanding these categories can help you change how you view yourself, how you view situations, and how you respond to the situations.

DOI: 10.4324/9781003308218-14

I am a firm believer that most people are more likely to hinder their own success than anyone else's. The space between our ears is the hardest battlefield for us to win. But once we have that corrected, there is not much you can't achieve.

Destructive self-talk causes you to question yourself so that you soon become paralyzed with doubt and uncertainty. You will become too critical of yourself, and the vicious cycle will continue.

Self-talk should be beneficial. It should be encouraging you to do your best and to be your best. For some people, self-talk is about identifying your purpose. What is it that you offer that no one else does? What talents or abilities do you bring to the table?

When you realize you do have assets to bring to your leadership role, then you need to encourage yourself often! Self-talk or the recorder shouldn't just be playing occasionally. It should be in constant loop mode, where you are continually telling yourself that you are awesome and you can do it! Your recorder or self-talk can influence as much as 99% of your success!

So, when the negative self-talk starts, take a timeout! Just like in a football or basketball game, if a team is performing poorly, they will call a timeout to regroup, assess the situation, and make adjustments to get back on track. You can do the same thing to get back on track as well. A few strategies to help include:

- ◆ Start the day with positive thoughts, such as what you are grateful for or a goal you accomplished yesterday.
- ◆ Surround yourself with positive people.
- ◆ Give yourself positive affirmations throughout the day.
- ◆ Give yourself a break when you do make a mistake.
- ◆ Say "I Don't" Instead of "I Can't." "Don't" means you are in control.
- ◆ Laugh and be in the moment.

I know you are expected to be the cheerleader for your staff and students, but don't forget to be your biggest cheerleader too. Everyone has shortcomings. Everyone has a bad day (or days, or weeks). Just don't let it get you down or let it become what you identify yourself with. Instead, feed yourself positivity all day, and call a time out if negativity starts to creep into your thinking. Remember you have talents and strengths that no one else has. Go make it an amazing day and amazing week, because you are amazing!

15

Lace Up Your Shoes

Coach John Wooden was probably the greatest basketball coach of all time. He finished his career by winning ten NCAA titles in his last 12 seasons before he retired. Because of his winning teams, he was able to recruit the best basketball players in the country to play for him.

What is interesting is that even though he had some of the most amazing athletes, he always started with the basics. Now, some may think the basics are dribbling or shooting, but that is not where he started. The first thing he taught his world class recruits was how to put on their socks and lace up their shoes. Why did he start there? Because he knew if socks aren't put on properly, then you are at greater risk of getting blisters on your feet. And we all know that a blister on your foot greatly limits what you are able to do and negatively impacts everything from walking, running, jumping, to even changing direction. It affects everything!

So, when you have high expectations of your teachers, staff, colleagues, or maybe even family members, remember that for them to truly excel, you have to provide the support and tools they need to be successful. **Sometimes it is the simple things in the process that make all the difference.** Never forget the importance of properly lacing your shoes!

But this is also to inspire you to never forget the little things in your pursuit of excellence. I know many administrators who had big goals and wanted to make an impact on their staff. But

DOI: 10.4324/9781003308218-15

if you don't get the little things right, then it is impossible to get the big things right.

And think of how much time we waste when we never get the little things right. I often ask leaders, how often do you address the same issues with your staff or students, or how often do you address the same issues at home. For instance, if you spend an hour every night trying to get a child to go to bed, or wake up in the morning, how much time is wasted in the course of a week, month, and year? Now, what if you had that extra hour to focus on something else? You see, the little things can add up quickly. And they can interfere with getting to the next level of relationships, career, or some other goals.

You may not have the position you want yet, or have achieved all that you desire, but that doesn't mean you won't get there. And you don't want to have something simple keep you from reaching your full potential. I heard a military commander speak several years ago, and he said the first thing to do every day is make your bed. He said excellence is about discipline and consistency. And as the commander said, even if you have a really bad day, at least you know you will have a nice, made-up bed to come home and fall into!

So, as you prepare your team for a great week or year, and all the game planning that you have done, don't forget to first help them lace up their shoes!

16

Make Yourself Accessible

Ever had an administrator, or maybe you are that administrator, who says they have an open-door policy? The open-door policy implies that your team members or colleagues can come to you with anything. That desire to be a transparent and available leader is admirable. The problem starts when people knock on the proverbial door and there is no answer. Or worse when you make time, but it is not quality time. So even more important than making yourself available is making yourself accessible.

When I say ACCESSIBLE, I don't just mean AVILABILE. Availability is about quantity of time, such as, "I will let you know what hours I am available in my office." **But accessibility is about the quality of time; it's about presence and focus.**

Being *available* is mainly a function of time management. Available leaders:

♦ Put team members and colleagues on their calendars to meet
♦ Leave time in their weekly calendar for unscheduled conversations

Being *accessible* is mainly a function of relationship. Accessible leaders:

♦ Make people feel at ease
♦ Encourage open and honest conversation

DOI: 10.4324/9781003308218-16

- Provide coaching and guidance
- Don't stand on title or hierarchy
- Seek feedback

I had the good fortune to interview Coach Bobby Bowden a few years before he passed away. He was the winningest coach in D1 football history and a living legend. The focus of our interview was servant leadership. He had many stories to share, and he explained how he felt his role wasn't just to coach but to help his coaches and players become better people in life. In fact, the discussion would often go back to his former coaches and players. What I found interesting and fitting to this topic of accessibility is that in all those years as a D1 coach and with all the success he obtained, he never changed his phone number or made it unlisted. He said he never knew when a former player or coach might need something from him, reach out to him for advice, or let him know what was going on their life. Imagine being fully accessible to all those you have led for half a century. That is a special kind of leadership!

Interestingly, it was one of his former players, Joe Ostaszewski, who called up coach Bowden and said he had a friend who wanted to discuss leadership with him. To which his reply was something along the lines of "Well dadgum, tell him to give me a call."

Never get too busy to be accessible to those you lead. And don't just make time for them, but make sure it is time well spent!

17

Never Give Up!

Earlier I shared that failure is a comma, meaning that it should not be seen as fatal or final. But I think it's important to also realize that you should have many commas in your career!

You don't have to get everything right all the time. But even when you fail miserably, and you will, that is no reason to give up.

Ironically, even the most basic skills, such as walking, have actually been fine-tuned through failure. As a toddler, did you stand up and walk perfectly on your first attempt? Did you just give up and decide to crawl the rest of your life? Of course not. You stumbled around like a drunk person, fell on your face, and stood back up (maybe even climbed back up) to repeat the process again.

Think of when you tried something new, such as snow skiing. Were you an expert on the first try? No, but if you are now a good skier, it is because you pushed yourself to try harder, even when you were falling more than you were actually skiing. Even an Olympic skier, like Lindsey Vonn, was not able to ski the first time she tried, but much like walking, she learned to become a world class skier. When she learned to ski, she didn't remain on the bunny slope either. She remained resilient as each level became more difficult. She would get up and try again.

There is an old adage that even an expert was once a novice. The only way to ultimately succeed is to push yourself beyond your comfort zone, be willing to take chances, and yes even fail.

DOI: 10.4324/9781003308218-17

In fact, expect it. **How many people failed to live up to their fullest potential because they were afraid to fail?** And how many people have failed to live up to their fullest potential because they weren't resilient in their failure to reflect and grow from it?

Excellence isn't taught, but rather it is developed through resilience and improving when you fail. While some people see failure as being fatal or the end of a dream, others see failure as part of the road to success. Some people say failure is not an option, but I say that failure is not optional; it is part of the process.

A now well-known man was once fired from a newspaper because the editor said he lacked creativity. This man failed on multiple occasions as an actor, entrepreneur, and even as an animator. This man, Walt Disney, had many failures before he created one of the most recognized names and brands in the world.

When asked about his success, Walt Disney focused on the fact that he had to overcome many obstacles, setbacks, and failures before he finally succeeded!

Walt was once quoted as saying, "Get a good idea, and stay with it. Dog it, and work at it until it's done, and done right." He picked himself up and learned from his mistakes and moved on. He said:

> To some people, I am kind of a Merlin who takes lots of crazy chances, but rarely makes mistakes. I've made some bad ones, but, fortunately, the successes have come along fast enough to cover up the mistakes. When you go to bat as many times as I do, you're bound to get a good average.
>
> (www.disneyhistoryinstitute.com/)

Now, this doesn't mean to accept any failure, especially if you didn't do your best. But when you give your best and it still comes up short, which it sometimes will, then just like Walt Disney, get back up, dust off, and get back in the batter box!

18

Knowledge Is No Longer Power

In the past, especially before the technology explosion, knowledge was power. For centuries, we all thought that was true. The basic management hierarchy of almost all organizations is based on that premise. This has been true in education as well. The top people in a school district know the vision and goals, and they share that down the line. Along these lines, knowledge becomes very powerful. In fact, in the past this knowledge was seen as power, and many tried to hold on to it as much as possible.

However, effective leaders find it more beneficial to pass along knowledge quickly so their teams can use that knowledge to make adjustments, changes, or move in a different direction if needed. So, speed of knowledge is important! In the information age, the world of knowledge is moving very fast. **There is no real need to keep most information to yourself as a leader.** Jason Jennings, best-selling author and speaker, shared an example of the he spent time with the Koch brothers discussing business leadership in his book, *Think Big, Act Small* (2005).

At the end of their visit, the CEO told him that he could take a copy of their five-year strategic plan to look over for any information that he needed. Jason asked, "Don't you want me to sign a non disclosure?" Charles replied, "No, in fact we send a copy of this out to our competitors to let them know how and when they are going to die." He was joking, of course, but his point was that

DOI: 10.4324/9781003308218-18

it is not the knowledge that makes them successful, but that it is the execution of it. Charles went on to tell him that he felt sorry for Jason because he was so old. And Jason replied, "What do you mean? I am not even as old as you."

Charles said,

> Only old people believe that knowledge is power. One time knowledge was power, when not everyone had access to it. But everyone has access to it now, so there is no need to try and keep from everyone. Especially within an organization. . . . It is not knowledge that is power now, but that flawless execution is power now. And the more people in your organization that have the knowledge or are 'In the know,' the more likely you are to have flawless execution, because everyone is on the same page.

Jason went on to share that he believes that in today's culture, knowledge kept in secrecy, or the holding on to knowledge, is the currency of the unproductive. These are the people who only have value because of the secrets they know. They are unproductive and they do very little, but people are afraid of them because they know all the secrets. I have worked with teachers like this in the past. I wondered how they kept their job, but realized they always knew the "secrets" and other teachers would often ask, "I wonder what they have on the administration?" You have probably worked with people like this as well.

So, the more transparent we are in sharing information, the less leverage there is for people to use or abuse that knowledge. Knowledge itself is not power. Rather than trying to hoard something that can be easily acquired, share your knowledge. Two people will collectively know more than one. Three will know more than two. And when you have a room full of smart people sharing their knowledge, there's very little you can't accomplish together. The flawless execution of knowledge is powerful.

19

Get Out of Your Comfort Zone

We hear a lot about getting out of our comfort zones to be successful. Phrases like "you have to be comfortable with being uncomfortable" are prevalent all over social media. However, if it were just that simple, I doubt we would see all the memes and quotes about the topic.

But in reality, this goes against how we are wired as humans. That is mainly because our brains are designed for survival, not for success. We do not like to do things that are uncomfortable or difficult. Our brains are designed to make life more comfortable and routine, to "play it safe."

Even when it comes to survival, our brains aren't really hardwired to focus on positive things that can help us be more successful. They are designed to focus on negative things as part of the survival instinct.

For example, imagine cavemen stepping out of their cave each morning and thinking, today I will discover fire or create the wheel. And even before they stepped out of the cave, they took a look in the mirror to give themselves some morning affirmations: I am great, I am wonderful, and everyone loves me.

No, instead they woke up, stepped outside, and immediately started looking for dinosaurs hiding behind trees to jump

DOI: 10.4324/9781003308218-19

out and eat them. They weren't focused on becoming successful, but on surviving. Since we are hardwired that way, most of us still think and react that way even in our technologically sophisticated age.

And the problem with a negative focus is that it affects all areas of our lives. For instance, you may get almost no credit for doing more than you promised to do, for going above and beyond or doing extra, but you get penalized severely for what you *don't* do.

As humans, we tend to:

◆ Remember traumatic experiences better than positive ones
◆ Recall insults better than praise
◆ React more strongly to negative stimuli
◆ Think about negative things more frequently than positive ones
◆ Respond more strongly to negative events than to equally positive ones

So, getting out of your comfort zone requires refocusing your energy away from the negative and toward more of the positive. It sounds easy, but as you see that is not how we are wired.

How can we reprogram our minds to focus on the positive and to move out of our comfort zones, to succeed rather than just survive?

◆ **Stop negative self-talk.** Make sure you are positive and uplifting to yourself.
◆ **Establish new patterns.** Change habits. Maybe go for walk, workout, read a book, or talk to family about good things that happened. Try new things.
◆ **Celebrate positive moments.** Don't be afraid to celebrate small successes.
◆ **Get a mentor.** Having someone to bounce ideas off of is important.

- **Learn a new skill/activity.** Be an example of a lifelong learner.
- **Do more public speaking.** Everyone is afraid of it!

Remember if you want to really be successful, you must change your focus and your habits. This is how you move out of your comfort zone. It is not always easy, but it will be well worth it when you do!

20

Connect Through Conflict

One of the most important skills of an administrator is the ability to handle conflict effectively. This is not only important for leaders, but for everyone professionally and personally. Conflict is often seen as a four-letter word to most of us. We are not comfortable with it, so we aren't very good at it. Because it is something we aren't very good at doing, we view it in a negative light. We would rather do almost anything than confront another person regarding an issue.

But whether we like it or not, even in the best school cultures, conflicts will arise from time to time. Conflict is kind of like stress. It's not that we will never encounter it, but it is how we deal with it that matters. While confronting someone is not really pleasant, it's something you must do as a professional, and how you do it makes all the difference.

One trait of effective leaders is that they are skilled in handling confrontations. And one of their main skills is creating an environment where teachers and staff feel safe to speak up. Many teachers by nature are highly agreeable so they avoid conflict as much as possible, even when they know they should speak up. Another reason is that it's a natural human reaction to shy away from disagreeing with a superior. So, I tell administrators when someone does speak up, realize that it may be very important for them to take the risk to do so.

Don't shy away from conflict when it arises, but rather use the opportunity to build stronger relationships with your

DOI: 10.4324/9781003308218-20

teachers. The reason confrontation is hard is that it is outside our comfort zones. We let things build until emotions are high, and then we tend to overreact. Here are some great strategies to help you deal with conflict better and actually make it a beneficial part of the communication process.

1. **Focus on being proactive, not reactive.** By this I mean don't wait on small issues to become large issues. Deal with them as soon as possible so they will be more manageable.
2. **Focus on relating, not being right.** Usually by the time we are willing to confront someone, we have let our emotions become overcharged. I like to say that we let things go until, "We have had it up to here"! But if we wait until this point, then we are more focused on winning an argument or on being right than we are about dealing with the actual issue.
3. **Focus on the issue, not on the individual.** Don't take it personally. Whether it is a student acting out, a teacher disagreeing with you, or whatever, don't see it as a personal attack on you. So, when dealing with the issue, rather than the individual, what we are saying is that you should focus on the behavior at the root of the conflict and not on the personality of the individuals.
4. **Focus on the future, not on the conflict.** One of two things results from conflict. Either there is some sort of compromise and a solution to the issue, or maybe there is no resolution and there has to be the "next steps" conversation. Hopefully, you reach a compromise more often than not. However, if there needs to be a next step, then that has to be addressed without a personality conflict. Make sure your teachers know that it is not personal and that correcting a problem or issue is all that matters to you.

The key to these "connecting through conflict" strategies working is for everyone to be on board and understand that this is the process. This will help curb the grapevine and put everyone on the same page. Just like a team needs shared values, and shared vision, they also need shared strategies for dealing with conflict. And remember not to see it as a bad or negative thing. After all, confrontation handled well has many benefits:

- Innovative solutions to problems
- Improvements to the status quo
- Stronger confidence in implementing ideas
- Stronger relationships
- Greater harmony
- Improved communication
- Better teamwork
- Greater understanding
- Increased engagement on the job

Remember, whether it is with personal or professional relationships, conflict will arise. But when it is handled correctly, there are many positive benefits that will actually help make the team even stronger!

21

Affect, Don't Infect

One thing I emphasize with leaders is to not let the negativity around them become part of them. Don't take your troubles home, and don't bring your troubles to school. I think this is especially true of leaders because their emotions are contagious. Whatever attitude you bring to school is likely to infect your whole staff. I like to say affect your staff, don't infect your staff.

This doesn't mean you are super cheery all the time. Life and school can be hard. But try not to let that bad day become days, or let those days negatively affect your leadership. **Remember, leadership is all about influence, and you as the leader have influence over the climate of the school or the classroom.**

There is an old tale of a carpenter who had a worry tree outside of his home where he would figuratively place his worries of the day before he entered into his home to be with his family. He said he might have troubles at work, but that doesn't mean his family needed to worry about them too, so he left them outside until morning. So, try as much as possible to leave your worries at the door when you walk into the school building each morning and focus on making a positive impact for the day. In fact, put a hanger there to symbolically leave them as you walk into the school.

Then when you get home, hang your professional worries outside before you walk in the door. This way you don't bring your work problems home for your family or friends to worry about.

DOI: 10.4324/9781003308218-21

As the story goes, the carpenter said the next morning when he picked up the worries, they were much lighter than when he left them.

As a leader, focus on lowering your stress and worries. Focus on taking care of yourself. We tell teachers to practice self-care, but leaders have to set the example. Learn to delegate to people with the strengths to do the job as well or maybe even better. Remember that you don't have to know everything, and it is okay to ask for help if needed. Finally, take care of your physical health. Stress is often manifested because of physical ailments, including a lack of restful sleep. So, focus on taking care of yourself so you can handle the stress. And if nothing else, learn to leave your worries at the door. You might just find them lighter when you return to them later!

22

Relationships Before Rigor, Grace Before Grades, Patience Before Programs, Love Before Lessons

Remember how education was thrown upside down when the pandemic first hit in March 2020? Teachers were expected to jump from a traditional school setting to the virtual world. I received messages from teachers all around the globe who were frustrated, stressed out, and in tears. Many were questioning their own ability and if they should even stay in teaching. Well, administrators were in the same boat of changing 100 years of education in a week or two. I felt educators needed some special encouragement, so I came up with the aforementioned quote to encourage them through it all. It was so well received by administrators and teachers across the country that it took on a life of its own.

Now years later, we are still experiencing the effects of the pandemic, and it is to some extent a different world now. But hopefully it will help us return to a more humanized perspective when it comes to education. Because somewhere along the way we became so focused on data and standardized test scores that we forgot the students and educators behind them.

This doesn't mean that we don't have high expectations, or that we expect less from those we lead. **It means that if you**

DOI: 10.4324/9781003308218-22

don't get the relationship right, then you will never get the best out of others. Remember that they are human first and when you focus on things like building relationships, patience, grace, and yes even love, they will actually work harder and be more successful. Students work harder for teachers they like and who care about them. It's also true that adults work harder for leaders who support, care for, and appreciate them.

Remember it is about the people you lead. It is about connecting and letting them know you have their best interests at heart. Let this quote be your motto for the year and the rest of your career! Relationships, patience, grace, and love will create a positive school culture where everyone will thrive!

23

Incorporate the Pygmalion Effect

If you have ever attended one of my workshops, you have already heard of the Pygmalion Effect. It is based upon the play where Professor Henry Higgins makes a bet that he can teach Cockney flower girl Eliza Doolittle how to speak proper English to fit in with the elites of society. It is a psychological phenomenon in which high expectations lead to improved performance.

I have often said that students will rise to the level of your lowest expectations, but the reality is that this is true of adults as well. I believe that high achievement is usually attained in the context of high expectations.

This was proved to an extent by Rosenthal and Jacobson (1968)[1], who conducted a study of all students in a single California elementary school. They were given a disguised IQ test at the beginning of the study. These scores were not disclosed to teachers. Teachers were told that some of their students (about 20% of the school chosen at random) could be expected to be "intellectual bloomers" that year, doing better than expected in comparison to their classmates. The bloomers' names were made known to the teachers. At the end of the study, all students were again tested with the same IQ test used at the beginning of the study. First and second graders showed statistically significant gains favoring the experimental group of "intellectual bloomers." This led to the conclusion that teacher expectations, particularly for the

DOI: 10.4324/9781003308218-23

youngest children, can influence student achievement. Rosenthal and Jacobson (1968) believed that even attitude or mood could positively affect the students when the teacher was made aware of the "bloomers." The teacher may pay closer attention to and even treat the child differently in times of difficulty.

While this first study focused on students, there have been many other studies which have focused on adults with the same results. In one study, conducted by the Israel Defense Forces (Eden, 1992),[2] an experiment was conducted on a sample of 105 men with at least 11 years of schooling, who had been selected into a combat command course on the basis of ability and motivation. Their instructors were four experienced training officers. Each instructed a group of about 25 trainees. Trainees were randomly listed as high, average, and low performing.

In the following training, it turned that when trainees were believed to be high performing, they did become high performing. Those who were believed to be low performing turned out to be low performing. The Pygmalion Effect also shows the biases of leaders. If they thought someone was high achieving, they gave them their best and when they thought someone was low achieving, they didn't give them their best. Best leadership is thus derived directly from high expectations.

In essence, the Pygmalion Effect is a type of self-fulfilling prophecy (SFP). Leaders who expect more of their subordinates lead them to greater achievement. How is this relevant to you as a principal? How you treat your staff largely determines their job performance. The best leaders create high performance expectations that the staff will fulfill.

As a leader, if you don't think a person can achieve a high level of success, then they probably won't. This doesn't necessarily mean that they aren't capable, but that you may not be using your best leadership skills when supervising them because you don't expect them to excel.

The bottom line is this:

◆ **Leaders,** believe in your team.
◆ **Hold positive and high expectations** that they will be successful, and they will often meet or exceed your expectations.

◆ **Be aware of how you are leading them.** If you don't have high expectations, then you may not be bringing your best leadership skills and thereby you are inhibiting their growth.

What we think of people, especially when we are in a position of authority, really does become a self-fulfilling prophecy. So, expect the best of those you lead, and you will give them your best, which will in fact help them be their best!

Notes

1   Rosenthal, R., & Jacobson, L. (1968). *Pygmalion in the classroom: Teacher expectation and pupils' intellectual development.* Holt, Rinehart & Winston.

2   Eden, D. (1992). Leadership and expectations: Pygmalion effects and other self-fulfilling prophecies in organizations. *The Leadership Quarterly, 3*(4), 271–305.

24

Small Talk Can
Have Big Benefits

I have often said that school administrators have the toughest job. They have to balance the mandates and expectations of the district with serving those they lead. Because of this balance, some leaders may not feel like they have time for small talk. They may feel like this is not the best use of their time. But as I have said many times and will continue to say, education is all about relationships. And not just between staff and students but between staff and administrators as well. It may be called small talk, but it plays no small role in our lives. The people who think we waste time talking about our family, cat, lunch, etc. don't understand that small talk is the structure relationships are built upon.

I have also gotten many messages from teachers who describe a similar situation where their administrators may pass them in the hall without even saying hello or acknowledging their existence, as some have put it. Now, I understand that they may have a lot on their mind or be in deep thought about something, but it makes the teachers and staff feel unappreciated or not valued. This is not a culture you want to create within a school.

So, as often as possible make time to interact with your staff about the little things going on in their classroom or in their lives

DOI: 10.4324/9781003308218-24

in general. In case you weren't aware, people like to talk about themselves and their lives. So, you can really connect with your staff by taking the time to listen. Ironically, I have been told more than once that I am a good conversationist, when in fact all I did was take time to listen to their stories.

Small talk is a gesture of respect. At the very least, it shows that you can take some sort of interest in someone's life and well-being, helping them feel both seen and heard – two things that we do not intentionally do enough. Further, small talk enables you to be more present.

Small talk also helps build trust. It is a gesture of spending time facing each other, exchanging pleasantries, and establishing that relationship. Nothing else is possible without this trust-building period.

Small talk can convey warmth and affection. I remember visiting a school once where the principal, a friend of mine, had a stern expression on his face for most of the visit. His expression wasn't warm and inviting even though he is a great guy and has a good sense of humor. He just seemed to be stressed and it showed in his expressions. I suggested that he smile more because it would make him feel better and it would help people be more comfortable approaching him. Smiling is Approachability 101 to engaging in small talk.

Finally, small talk shows them that you value them as a person and not just as a professional. It is one of the best ways to establish rapport, communicate needs, get information, and establish relationships. So, go out of your way to have personal exchanges with your employees and co-workers. You don't need to build friendships, but there's no reason why you can't get to know each other. **Personal working relationships are important for cultivating a sense of team, and if people see you as another person on the team, they'll be more receptive when you disclose your ideas or opinions.** The key here is to seem imperfect, approachable, and human. One way I kept that approachable side was to always inquire about events in my teachers' lives. If a child or family member was sick or maybe someone was graduating or getting married, I would ask about them. Teachers appreciate it when you treat them as humans with lives outside of school, and not just as the teacher in the classroom.

As you begin this week, remember that small talk may lead to larger conversations and deeper connections with your staff and a more positive team culture!

25

Put Teachers First

Putting teachers first is a concept that is dear to me. So much so that I wrote a book (*Putting Teachers First: How to Inspire, Motivate, and Connect with Your Staff*, 2018) about it. I know it is almost heresy for someone not to say the students come first. But the reality is that putting teachers first should be the focus of school leadership. This has nothing to do with importance, but priorities.

If you ask a marriage counselor, they will say that the spouse always comes first. Interestingly, research shows that putting your spouse first actually provides the security, comfort, and stability that helps children thrive.

If this is the case at home, then it stands to reason that the same is true at school as well. And many leaders have probably never thought of it in this context, but how they treat their teachers and staff is observed and even modeled by students. If students see teachers are not appreciated and treated poorly, then why would they treat them any differently? They would be, after all, reflecting how they see other adults treating their teachers.

But what if students saw their teachers respected, appreciated, and treated like highly qualified professionals? Wouldn't they be just as likely to model that behavior as well? A lot is said of respect in the classroom, but it is respect shown and given before even getting to the classroom that is even more important. Wouldn't this also encourage teachers and staff to be more trusting and

DOI: 10.4324/9781003308218-25

supportive of you as a leader? Because I can tell you that being a leader can be isolating at times, and when you feel the support of your staff, it can make a huge difference in your ability to be a more effective leader.

Research has shown that effective school leadership is among the strongest predictors of teacher retention. How principals engage their teachers matters in terms of whether they will stick around. In workshops, I tell administrators that students shouldn't be the only reason teachers want to stay; they should be one of the reasons too.

And it is not just about maintaining consistency with low turn-over, which is important. It is also about the culture and morale. Did you know that Gallup research shows when teachers feel like they are valued and that their strengths are being utilized, that they are 6 times more engaged at work (Flade, Asplund, & Elliot, 2015)[1]?

Yes, you heard right, 6 times more engaged! They are also 3 times more likely to report having an excellent quality of life and 15% less likely to quit their job.

So, in a sense, morale is actually a reflection of leadership. Leaders need to ensure that teachers feel supported, encouraged, and appreciated so that morale is high, but also so that you get the best from your staff. It is an old adage, but remember that the student learning environment is also the teacher working environment.

So, if it is really about the students, then make sure it is about the teachers and staff too. After 30 years in education, I can assure you that when administrators take care of their staff, their staff will go above and beyond to take care of the students.

Note

1   Flade, P., Asplund, J., & Elliot, G. (2015). Employees who use their strengths outperform those who don't. *Gallup News*. https://www.gallup.com/workplace/236561/employees-strengths-outperform-don.aspx

26

Hold Aspirational Conversations

There has been a push over the past decade to toughen teacher evaluations. Billions of dollars were spent on implementing high-stakes teacher evaluation systems in nearly every state. The belief was that it would greatly improve student achievement.

However, research shows that those efforts failed: Teacher evaluation reforms over the past decade had no impact on student test scores or educational attainment. You read that correctly. They have had no impact, well, except the negative impact placed on teacher morale.

If there is a lesson to be learned here it is that teachers are professionals and that treating them less than professionally is of no benefit to the school and especially to student achievement. Hopefully this data will change how some districts evaluate teachers. Could it possibly be time to follow high performing countries such as Finland where they don't even have a formal teacher evaluation? Since we are so data driven in education, maybe this is the data we need to change how we evaluate teachers. **Instead of always looking for what teachers need to improve, maybe we can focus on strengthening what they do well.**

I have often said that we hire teachers for their strengths, yet we manage them based on their weaknesses. The irony of most hiring is that we seek out candidates who will bring value to the

DOI: 10.4324/9781003308218-26

position. We look for people with a strong resume and talents that stand out. However, once we have this perfect candidate in place, the focus becomes more about improving performance or fixing weaknesses than it is about improving the strengths on which they were hired.

I remember my first year of teaching in a very large school system. I was looking forward to bringing my talents and strengths to my new job. However, within the first few weeks of school, I was given something called a PAC, which was a personal appraisal cycle that was meant for me to focus on areas of improvement for the school year. So, I was basically required to spend my first year of teaching focusing on two or three areas that I felt needed improvement. This is not a unique situation when you consider that most employees are evaluated with a perform-ance review, which usually focuses on areas of improvement or areas of growth, which is just a nice way to say weaknesses.

The normal evaluation is usually called the sandwich, where you say one nice thing, then you add on layers of improvements and areas of growth, then end with one nice thing. I have also heard it called the kiss, kick, kiss process. And guess how the teachers usually leave the evaluation? Yes, feeling like they have been kicked a lot.

After nearly 30 years in education, I can tell you that most teachers are their own worst critics. They are constantly reflecting on what they don't do well. It is how they have been conditioned. So, using the old traditional methods of evaluation really do little for teacher improvement. In Finland, where they don't even have a formal teacher evaluation, they trust that their teachers are professionals and that they are self-aware enough to know when they need support.

What strengths does your staff bring? If we think of the staff like a team, then we need people with different talents and skills. For instance, if we were creating a sports team, everyone can't be the quarterback, or the running back, and not everyone can be a receiver. The key to success is to put people in positions where they can be most effective. Then look for other opportunities for them to grow even more, especially if they are seeking out new opportunities.

Finally, we need to hire for strengths, and we need to manage for strengths. This means that we don't just evaluate teachers, but we treat them as professionals who are looking to maximize their strengths and potential. I suggest instead of the traditional evaluation or an end of the year evaluation that you include aspirational conversations. These conversations help you understand the goals and needs of each staff member to really help them be the best teammate possible.

There are several key questions to ask staff on a regular basis or during a formal evaluation which give a voice to your teachers and show them that you view them as professionals. I have included five questions as examples, but you can be creative and add more or change them to best fit your school culture.

Questions to Ask During Aspirational Conversations:

1. Have we helped you be successful?
2. What do you think we do well? (such as reading, extra-curricular, etc.)
3. What do you see, such as in other schools, that would make us do better?
4. What would make you want to leave us?
5. What are your professional goals? How can we help you achieve them?

People often leave because they're not valued and because there is no room to grow. Does someone desire to work towards an administrative role? Or maybe take on different role in the school? Tell them you will help them get there. Value them by letting them know that if they are the best teacher they can be every day, then you will help them achieve their professional goals. It is important to remember that teachers create the climate in which students learn – and when teachers feel valued and supported, they create dynamic learning environments.

27

No More Buts!
Leave Buts Behind

One of the most important jobs of a leader is build strong, positive relationships. As I have mentioned many times, this begins with small talk – listening and learning about those you lead. Another important aspect of the job, if not the most important, is inspiring, motivating, and praising those you lead. I have always believed there should be about a 6:1 ratio of positive comments to negative comments to be most effective as a leader.

Chester Elton (NY Times Best Selling author) shared with me in an interview about the former CEO of Avis car rental, Carlos Aguilera. Carlos would make a habit of visiting car rental places around the country. He would put ten pennies in his pocket and during the course of the day he would give compliments and praise to his staff and move a penny to the other pocket. That way he knew he gave at least ten positive compliments each day. This is great for two reasons. One, he was focused on giving positive feedback or praise, and second, it meant he had to spend time with his employees. He wasn't tucked away in his CEO office.

This is why I think it is so important for principals and assistant principals to spend time in the classrooms. Don't just show up for a formal evaluation, but make sure you frequently drop by informal observations or just to visit the class.

DOI: 10.4324/9781003308218-27

And when you do, make sure you leave them with a compliment or praise, but leave the "buts" behind. How often have you seen, or experienced yourself, a quick observation where the administrator tells you "Good job," and instead of leaving it there, the administrator just *has* to add a "but . . ." They feel like they aren't doing their job unless they include a quick critique. The problem, however, is that the "but" negates the praise. And guess which one the teacher will focus on the rest of the day? That's right, the criticism! **This isn't to say that you should never critique a teacher or give honest feedback. But building teachers up on what they do well should always be the focus.** So, I recommend you give the praise but leave the buts behind. Give them feedback that is:

1. **Timely:** Recognition is a powerful, positive way to reinforce action or behaviors you want to see again and again, but that power is diluted the longer you wait to recognize someone.
2. **Specific:** There isn't much more wasteful or in some ways insulting than giving generic praise. "You did a great job in class today!" What does that mean? What did they do great? Be detailed in what they did that was great!
3. **Sincere:** You also need to be sincere. All praise must be based on a true appreciation of, and excitement about, the other person's success. Otherwise, your thanks may come across as manipulative rather than genuine.
4. **Frequent:** Recognition should never be viewed as a "one-and-done" task or something you put on your calendar to do on a monthly basis. Just as recognition should be timely, it should also occur every time you see exceptional behaviors, actions, or outcomes. Remember the CEO who kept pennies in his pocket to remind him to say a certain number of positive things each day? Use pennies or whatever it takes to get in the habit of praising your teachers.
5. **Recognize Effort, Not Just Results:** We are used to rewarding results. If someone achieves a goal, then we reward it. However, if we truly value innovation and

curiosity, then we have to recognize *effort* as well. We know that not everything a teacher tries will be successful, but this doesn't mean that the effort shouldn't be recognized. In fact, when we focus on accountability or results, then we lose sight of innovation and outside the box thinking, which are the traits we hope to instill in our students, not just our teachers.

When I would visit classrooms, or do an informal observation, I would always leave a Post-it note with a specific point of praise. At times, I would even leave a note on the board if a classroom were empty, just to leave a note of encouragement or to tell the class how lucky they were to have their teacher.

Because it's not just notes from students that teachers love and cherish; it is notes of praise and appreciation from their administrators as well.

28

Every Day Is a New Beginning

One of the most effective coaching and even teaching strategies is to let every day be a fresh new start. This is important for you, for your staff, and for your students, especially if yesterday was an off or bad day. Now, I could probably call this having a short-term memory, because it is really the same mindset, but the idea is that we all make poor choices or have bad days but that doesn't mean we can't move on from them. We so often let mistakes get us down and become our focus. That is our second mistake, putting too much focus on the mistake.

I think in education and especially in administration, there is a false notion that we have to be on and giving 110% at all times. That we can never make mistakes and when we do, then all heck breaks loose. Then we become our own worst critics, beating ourselves up over it.

What is ironic is that we have been trained to some extent to show grace to students when they mess up. For instance, have you ever had a student who acted out or just seem frustrated, but it was out of character for them? Some of them worry about whether or not you will still like them. One of the first things I would tell students at the beginning of the year was that I have high expectations, but I that I don't take it personally if you don't always live up to them. You may have consequences to an action, but every day is a new day in the classroom. Imagine how comforting it can be to some students just to know you aren't going to take things personally!

DOI: 10.4324/9781003308218-28

We need to do this with our colleagues as well. There were days as a teacher, administrator, and even now where I just fail miserably. We don't like to use the term fail, but sometimes it just fits. And that's okay, because we all fail.

I had a principal early in my AP career who didn't like handling conflict. For instance, when a teacher was frequently tardy, he wouldn't have a conversation with the teacher, but rather he called an early morning meeting and made a sweeping comment about how we were supposed to at school at certain time and it was unprofessional to be late. I kid you not, the teacher wasn't at the meeting, so the intended person wasn't even there. But guess how the teachers who did attend felt? Yes, their morale was crushed. We had a good relationship with the principal, so I shared with him how the teachers felt, because they told me, and he realized that he had basically failed!

Fortunately, our failures are not fatal. **We get the chance to start anew every day, just like we do with students in our schools.** Always be forward focused, on new goals, new hopes and dreams. Give yourself a little grace and don't hold grudges against yourself for not always being perfect. I have often heard that hope is not a strategy, and while it may not be, it does give us the opportunity to look past our mistakes. Learn to let some things go, and look ahead because every day is a new beginning!

29

Know Your Worth?

While that has become almost cliché for people to say in our culture, it really is important for you to know your worth! The reason the quote has a question mark is this: When was the last time you thought about your worth? Especially as a leader, you get caught up in the busyness of the day and you may not give much thought to what all you are contributing to your school, staff, students, or community in general.

Another reason we don't reflect on our worth is that our culture and field of education are so focused on weaknesses. We evaluate teachers and the focus is often on areas of improvement, or areas of growth. We do the same with students, when we focus on areas in which they need to improve instead of areas that they do well. Even as an administrator, the focus from the district level may be on areas of growth for you or especially for the school. We feel like we always have to be critiquing and because of that, we sometimes forget what we do well. **If we as a society and as an educational system focused more on our talents than on our weaknesses, we would all feel more valuable.**

Here are four tips to help you know your worth.

1. **Although it is easier said than done, don't compare yourself to others.** When you stop comparing yourself to others, you can begin to focus on your own unique path, your goals, and what you personally value in life. I have always found it interesting that when we compare

DOI: 10.4324/9781003308218-29

ourselves to others, it is to those we think are better off than we are. We rarely compare ourselves to the millions of people who would love to be in our shoes.

2. **Focus on serving and helping others.** When we give of ourselves to others it is an amazing feeling. There are many ways to give back and help others. When you meet someone and find yourself comparing or judging, shift your mentality to one of service. Ask yourself, "How can I serve this person?" You will be amazed with how many opportunities emerge when we start thinking this way. When we decide to focus on serving others, we begin to think positively and feel good about ourselves.

3. **Be talent- or strength-focused.** We often know what we don't do well, but we rarely think of what we do well. It's like if there is a group of colleagues, such as administrators, or teachers, they can tell you the strengths of their teammates, but we often struggle to see what we do well, what adds to our value. It is not just coincidence that the term "talent" is actually a unit of value or worth and in the past was a name given to money. So, in reality our talents are a big part of what gives us our value. Take time to recognize your talents and strengths because they reflect your worth or value.

4. **It's more than "just be yourself."** I think "just be yourself" is true. Don't try to be something you are not, and you certainly shouldn't try to be like someone else. But I think it is a little more than that. I think the key is to "be yourself with skill," or "be your best self." This means that you are staying true to who you are and the talents, abilities you possess, but you are working to get the most out of them.

When you realize your worth, it helps you recognize the difference you make in the world!

30

Use the Handwritten Note

One of the things I enjoy about traveling around the country speaking at schools is that I get to meet amazing teachers and amazing administrators. I have often said that when I walk into a school, I can tell quickly about the climate of the school and the effectiveness of the leadership by how everyone interacts. That is because while we know education is a fulfilling job, it is also a very hard job! While there is more to building culture than just a first impression, a first impression is all some people ever get so it does make a difference. It affects how the office staff interacts with visitors, students, staff, and even each other. It affects how staff interact in the hallways and whether people seem happy to be there.

Now I have to admit that most schools I enter have an awesome administration, otherwise they probably wouldn't invite me to their school in the first place. I am a teacher advocate, and they know this upfront. But even within these schools, there are some leaders who really stand out. And it is always a reflection of the leadership. The leaders understand that education is a hard job, and that teachers and staff need all the support and encouragement they can get.

Because it is a hard job, it is important for teachers and staff to feel like they are appreciated for their hard work. **It is important that every person feels seen, heard, and acknowledged as an individual, not just as a collective team.** And one of the best ways to make them feel acknowledged is to communicate with them personally. We have become such a high tech, texting, email, and instant message culture, that we have forgotten what a quick handwritten note or handwritten letter can do to lift someone's spirit. I always encourage principals and assistant principals to keep Post-it notes with them and leave notes for teachers throughout the school.

One of my favorite things as an administrator was visiting classrooms and watching amazing teachers in action. When I left, I would leave a Post-it note on their desk telling them how lucky their students were to have them and share something I learned or enjoyed about the visit.

Yes, teachers love notes and drawings from students, but they also love notes of appreciation from their administrators. When I share a tweet on this topic, I always get many responses of teachers who say they keep those notes and love looking back on them when they have a tough day!

And don't make it a one-time thing. Getting little notes throughout the year is a great morale booster and lets people know you see them and appreciate them. Every educator I know keeps these and cherishes these like treasures, because, well, they are treasures. While it may sound cliché, I have found that when it comes to life, people, and experiences, it is the little note of encouragement and praise that helps refill their cups and keep them going!

31

Be Fully Present

I was the closing keynote for the Oklahoma Association of Elementary Principals this past week, and I had a principal share with me afterwards that she really loved what I shared and one point really stuck out. It was about being fully present. She said with all the multitasking that a leader has to do, that we do sometimes forget to be as fully present in the moment as possible.

For instance, have you ever attended a meeting and said "present" when they called your name, but then for most of the meeting, you weren't really present or at least you weren't fully present? Or have you asked for a meeting with someone, like a teacher or even your administrator, and they spent most of their time checking their phone, or preoccupied with something else?

There is a difference between being present and being fully present. This is not just true in school but in our everyday life as well. For instance, we always like to talk about being in the moment, but the reality is that most people are only paying full attention in the present moment, 50% of the time. That means we basically miss out on half our life, with our attention somewhere other than in the moment.

It is important to be in the moment, to be fully present with your teachers, staff, and even students. I can't tell you the number of messages I get from teachers who say they wish their administrators would slow down and really listen to them – to take an extra moment in the hallway when they ask, "How are you" to really listen to the answer. You never know what you

DOI: 10.4324/9781003308218-31

may be missing if you are just going through the motions or your mind is elsewhere. Leaders, when you meet with teachers or staff, make sure to set enough time aside to be fully present with them. If you aren't fully engaged, then they feel you don't value them or their time, when that may not be the case at all. I know you have busy schedules, so instead of asking someone to "make it quick," just schedule a time to meet with them later. And then make sure that time is solely focused on them. I don't like when I am speaking to someone and they are on the phone, texting, or doing something else instead of engaging with me. Most people feel this way, so no cell phone, laptop, or anything else to distract you. Just you and them and direct eye contact and full attention. It will make them feel more valued and will help you understand the situation and make better decisions.

Finally, learn to be focused on the moment whether you are at school or home. It can be easy to be on autopilot with your day-to-day schedule, but it is important to spice it up a bit each day so that you are able to actually enjoy the present. We are creatures of habit and often when we are in the "fray of the day," we turn on autopilot. And in those instances, we don't fully engage. Giving your full attention means you value the people or the activities in which you are engaged. So, don't just carpe diem, but carpe diem to the fullest!

32

Bring Out Their Best

Did you know the term "educate" comes from the root word "educere," which means to lead or draw out? We used to view education like the filling of a bucket, where we pour information and knowledge into the student. Then Yeats came along and said it's not the filling of a bucket, but it is the lighting of a fire. But the reality is that the optimal definition of education is when we lead or draw out the talents, passions, and abilities within each student. It literally means to bring out the greatness within. This is not only true of students, but adults as well. Leadership in its most effective form is to bring out the best in those you lead.

This is no more true than in education itself. I have often said we hire teachers based on their talents or strengths, but then we manage them based on their weaknesses. This may be the most ineffective management technique ever used. I jokingly ask principals when I do workshops if any of them have ever hired a teacher because they sucked really bad and you wanted to help improve their weaknesses. They of course smile or laugh and say no. That's because we hire them based on their strengths, and if that is why we want them in our schools, then those should be the areas we want them to develop even more.

The irony of all this is that we seek out candidates who will bring value to the position. We look for people with a strong resume and talents that stand out. However, once we have this perfect candidate in place, the focus becomes more about finding

DOI: 10.4324/9781003308218-32

and fixing weaknesses than it is about improving the strengths on which they were hired.

I remember my first year of teaching in a large school system. As I mentioned earlier, within the first few weeks of school, I was given something called a PAC, which was a personal appraisal cycle that I was supposed to use to focus on areas of improvement for the school year. It's true that most employees have to do performance reviews. But you can imagine how deflating that can be when that is your focus for the year. Yes, we all have areas we can work on and improve, but when they become the focus, how can we push, grow, and maximize our potential?

What strengths do your staff bring? **If we think of the staff like a team, then we need people with different talents and skills.** For instance, if we were creating a sports team, everyone can't be the quarterback, or the running back, and not everyone can be a receiver. The key to success is to put people in positions where they can be most effective. Then look for other opportunities for them to grow even more, especially if they are seeking out new opportunities.

Finally, we need to hire for strengths, and we need to manage for strengths. This means that we don't just evaluate teachers, but we treat them as professionals who are looking to maximize their strengths and potential. Let's get back to real education, which is bringing out the best in those we teach and lead!

33

Honk if You . . .

Don't you love all the bumper stickers that say, "Honk if you love . . ."? The subjects vary from cats, dogs, cheese, to even "Honk if you love honking"! What's even more humorous is that if someone were to honk at the bumper sticker, it may make the person angry because they forget it's even on their car.

But the honking I am referring to is not for bumper stickers, but the honking of geese in flight. Have you ever wondered why you can hear a team of geese honking when they are flying through the air? And yes, they are called a team in flight. One reason they honk is to make sure each one stays in formation because you know someone will be looking off in the wrong direction and fall out of formation. Fortunately, it feels the drag and resistance of trying to go it alone and quickly gets back into formation to take advantage of the lifting power of the team. So, this type of honking is important to make sure everyone is working toward the same goals and doing their part.

However, the main reason that geese honk is to encourage those around them to keep going. While it may seem insignificant, the reality is that even some animals understand the importance of encouragement and cheering each other on. Imagine if you created a culture in your school where everyone was supportive and encouraging to each other. It can be an instant culture changer. And what is interesting is that no matter which goose is out in the lead, the rest of the team is supporting and encouraging it until it tires, and then another one will take the heavy load.

DOI: 10.4324/9781003308218-33

While you would think we would work better as a team of geese, it seems we often have a hard time doing so in schools. But imagine if administrators and teachers all supported and encouraged each other? When is the last time you verbally encouraged your teachers, staff, colleagues, or even students? Don't be afraid to speak up and speak out to let others know you appreciate them and to encourage them. **Hopefully your team is working toward the same goals – a little honking just may be what they need to keep going strong!**

When I share this concept during professional development, I say that I expect to walk in their school tomorrow and hear everyone honking – honking encouragement to each other and pushing each other to do their best for themselves and the team!

34

The Best Team Wins!

The principalship may be one of the most isolating professions. You often feel stuck between the board and your staff. That you are out on an island alone trying to connect the two.

As an administrator, I always valued teamwork as much as a stellar teacher. That's because if greatness is performed in isolation, it does little to cultivate a dynamic school culture. But if you have a team of committed teachers to support, encourage, and motivate each other, that's a game changer! In fact, the best performing schools typically have the best functioning teams as well. This is because they are good at communicating, teamwork, and helping each other out. In poor performing schools, teachers often see asking for help as a sign of weakness, feel they will be judged, or feel like others wouldn't think they are doing their fair share.

Understanding your role as an influencer is the beginning of becoming an effective principal and creating a dynamic team culture! The key to a high performing team is an effective school leader. **You cannot administrate a school to excellence, but you can lead a school to excellence**.

Unfortunately, not every staff is a team, but as an effective leader, influencer, you have to create a sense of shared visions and goals. Then make sure you value every member for the talents they bring to the team and celebrate the talents they bring.

DOI: 10.4324/9781003308218-34

Administrators should create an environment where team-work is encouraged and the norm. It takes the whole team to be excellent. When you develop a team mindset, there is:

♦ Respect/trust for all members
♦ Willingness to share ideas/resources
♦ Common goals/vision
♦ Responsibilities based on strengths
♦ Effective leadership
♦ Everyone is supported/valued
♦ Everyone sees each other as colleagues, not competition

Finally, never forget that effective leaders understand that teachers know what their students (and what they themselves) need to succeed. So, be willing to elicit input and feedback from your staff to create a sense of team! In education, as in sports, it is not the best group of people that wins, but it is the best *team* that wins!

35

Don't Just Leave an Impression; Have an Impact!

We make impressions upon people every day. How we look, how we talk, even how we dress can all make an impression upon someone. But how often do you make an impact? What is the difference between *impression* and *impact*?

An impression is a vague notion, remembrance, or perception of someone. An impact, on the other hand, is to actually create a change in yourself or someone else.

Impressions are more temporary and superficial than an impact. But it is the one we are trained to focus on. Think about the old adage, "You only get one chance to make a first impression." We feel this pressure when we interview for a job, go on a date, or stand in front of our class on the first day. But impressions can change and even be forgotten (thank goodness!) over time because they are more temporary. **For leaders, leaving an impact means having a strong and positive effect on someone**.

Most of you got into education because of a teacher who impacted your life. Many teachers may have left an impression on you, such as being funny, a good listener, or genuinely caring, but the ones you remember best made some kind of impact. They were the ones who taught you to believe in yourself, celebrated your successes, genuinely cared for you, and even told you that you had talents and abilities to be successful. Some of us were greatly impacted by an administrator as well. In my book

DOI: 10.4324/9781003308218-35

Principal Bootcamp, I explain the impact that my high school principal had on me while I was still in high school.

He would greet students and teachers as they entered the school each morning. He would take time to talk and listen in the hallways and the cafeteria. He would step into classes just to see what was going on without a teacher evaluation in sight. Not that I would have recognized a teacher evaluation form, but he usually just had the two-way radio (yes, this was before cell phones) in his hand. He seemed to know every student, every parent, and connected with his teachers in a very caring way. He never seemed to be too stressed, even though I know some of the students, parents, and yes probably some teachers caused him to turn gray prematurely.

Years later, when I took my first administrative role, I recalled how he created such a family type culture, and I knew that was what I wanted to create as well. I also remembered him telling me during my senior year that I was one of the most talented students he had ever had and that I needed to use those talents to reach my fullest potential. Although I haven't heard from him in years, I hope that our paths may still cross again one day, so I can let him know the impact that he had on my professional career.

Be that administrator for your teachers and staff. Never get so focused on the process of leading that you forget the ones you are actually leading. Yes, it's important to make a first impression, but it's so much more important to have a lasting impact!

36

Know Your Personal Mission Statement

Have you ever wondered why your school has a mission statement? Or why you have to meet and discuss it every year? The purpose is to have a roadmap toward goals that help fulfill the purpose of the school. If mission statements are important for schools and businesses, then shouldn't we have them for our own lives? A personal mission statement can help you identify your values and goals, define what matters most to you professionally or even personally, and define a path to fulfilling your purpose. Now hopefully it is not like the many school mission statements that hang on the wall and are never given much attention shortly after being created.

When I speak to educators now, one of my points is to help them think of themselves as a business. Think about it, if you are a business, then what is the purpose of the business? What is your purpose? How do you know if you are achieving your purpose without a set of goals or a mission statement to help you stay on track? **I believe many people fall short of their best because they don't** *plan* **to be their best.**

Some examples of mission statements include, "To encourage, engage, and equip others to believe in themselves." "To positively impact the life of every person I lead." "To encourage everyone I interact with on a daily basis." And, of course, my personal mission statement has been simplified over time to

DOI: 10.4324/9781003308218-36

be . . . "Help educators maximize their talents professionally and personally to reach their full potential!"

So, as you think about your own mission statement:

1. Write down what's most important to you; identify core values.
2. Identify and articulate your most important goals.
3. Identify the legacy you want to leave.

Then create daily, weekly, short-term, and long-term goals that help guide your mission and help you live out your purpose. When you think about life in this manner, you will live not just like a person with a mission, but like a person on a mission! You'll set goals and crush them!

37

Remember Maslow
Before Bloom

We hear a lot lately about Maslow before Bloom when it comes to our students, but guess what, when it comes to teachers, they need Maslow before Bloom as well. Teachers need to feel safe, like they belong, and that their emotional needs are met. While it is everyone's responsibility to create a positive and supportive school culture, the principal has the most influence on the school environment. This is where you can build equity with your staff. And there's no better investment than leaders willing to build positive relationships with their staff.

First, put your staff at ease. An approachable leader makes people feel comfortable and at ease. People at ease can work together, connect, and communicate without fear of retribution. I remember one principal I had early in my career who would purposely send vague emails to teachers to meet at the end of the day. Teachers would be worried the rest of the day about the meeting, even if they had done nothing wrong. The principal said he did it because he wanted to keep teachers on their toes, but I knew it was just a way to control them with the fear of the unknown. I can't imagine treating teachers so unprofessionally. I would rather have teachers feel at ease than to have them worried about some mind games. As a principal, learn to be kind, gentle, and caring to your staff. Even if this doesn't come easy to you, it is something that you can develop much like your emotional intelligence. They are professionals, after all, who pour their heart and souls into their job, so be mindful of this and make sure you let them know how much you appreciate them and their commitment.

Teachers by nature speak the language of affirmation. This is why most teachers call their job a calling as much as a profession. **So, move beyond seeing teachers based on their titles or roles, and see them as humans who also need affirmation.** As leaders, it's easy for our focus to be on what we want to accomplish or what matters most urgently in the moment. Unfortunately, this can lead us to treat our employees as more of a means to an end than as valued contributors to our school's vision or long-term goals. Teachers, in reality, are your most valuable resource. You need to care for them.

Remember to do the little things like learn their names quickly. Ask about their children, family, or even their pets. People love to talk about themselves and the people important to them. And remember to ask them the two key questions often: "How are you?" and "How can I help you?" I hope you realize just how powerful those two questions can be. These will keep communication lines open and give you the opportunity to really listen and help.

It is important to have a warm demeanor, kind words, and a down to earth approach rather than be dismissive or discouraging. It is also important to be caring and compassionate. When teachers realize you truly care about them, then you have captured their heart. This is the highest level of connection that you can obtain in the workplace. It may not be surprising that those who perceive greater affection and caring from their leaders or even colleagues perform better. A longitudinal study by Sigal Barsade and Olivia A. O'Neill (2014)[1] showed that employees who felt they worked in a loving, caring culture reported higher levels of satisfaction and teamwork. They showed up to work more often. The research also demonstrated that this type of culture related directly to improved mood, quality of life, and overall satisfaction.

The more love teachers feel at school, the more engaged they are. This companionate love, which is far less intense than romantic love, is based on warmth, affection, and connection rather than passion. It is the small moments such as a warm smile, a kind note, and a sympathetic ear day after day that help create and maintain a strong culture of companionate love, and the staff satisfaction and commitment that come with it. It is all but impossible to capture their heart if you are focused on administrating, but you will almost certainly capture their heart by being a selfless leader.

Note

1   Barsade, S., & O'Neill, O. A. (2014, November 2). Employees who feel love perform better. *Harvard Business Review*. Retrieved December 13, 2022, from https://hbr.org/2014/01/employees-who-feel-love-perform-better

38

Be Visible

In the military, AWOL means Absent Without Leave. Based on the circumstances, it can result in a fine and confinement, or even lead to a discharge. In leadership, AWOL could be defined as Absent Without Leader. For some teachers this is a good thing, and they relish when their principal isn't in the building. But that should not be the case. You have to have such a great relationship with your staff that they want you to be present and accounted for!

The reality is that one of the most important attributes of a leader is that they are actually present. How odd would it be if you went to the orchestra and the conductor wasn't on stage? How would the music sound? Or what if a football team started a game without their coach? Would they know what to do? While you DO NOT want to micromanage your staff, you do want to be there to support and mentor your team.

It's hard to be invisible if you are in the trenches with your team as much as possible. Remain visible and approachable through the school day. The principal should NOT be hard to find. Instead of being tucked away in the office, be out in the school. Be in the hallways to interact with teachers and students throughout the day. This may not seem like a good use of time, but it is more important than you think. **From the teacher's perspective, the principals who lead are the principals who are seen.**

Greet students and their parents in the morning as they arrive and get out of cars or greet students as they step off the bus. Chat with the parents and bus drivers. Ask good questions,

DOI: 10.4324/9781003308218-38

then listen and learn from the responses. Ask about needs, potential problems, or brewing issues. While showing visibility, the multitasking principal at the same time demonstrates concern for others' welfare. That time invested in collecting information can prevent concerns from escalating and trouble from developing. You may find out about a student who may be having issues or is experiencing family problems. A proactive leader can head off a lot of situations before they become problems, simply by being present.

Teachers and students alike need to feel like their school administrators are active members of the day-to-day school community. You provide a send of safety, security, normalcy, and even calmness in a chaotic world. Here are a few more ideas of how to be seen throughout the day, while positively influencing the school culture.

- ◆ **Make morning announcements.** This is a great time to recognize accomplishments, celebrate successes, catch people being good, provide necessary information, and establish expectations. For children, the principal's voice conveys security, stability, and reassurance.
- ◆ **Cover for a teacher.** Offering your services as a guest teacher to model techniques and engage with students.
- ◆ **Be available in the hallways during transition times.**
- ◆ **Serve food in the cafeteria.** Help serve food or pass out milk during lunch. Observe kids' behavior in a less structured environment. Reinforce your expectations of manners and cooperation and that you are a servant leader.
- ◆ **Join different groups of staff and students for lunch.** Listen, learn, and get a pulse for what is happening in the school.
- ◆ **Attend extra-curricular events.** Let students know you care about them as a person and not just a student. Be there to support them as they show off their passions and talents.
- ◆ **Frequent the playground.** What a great opportunity to see students in their natural habitat, running, playing,

and having fun. This is also a great time to take a walk and chat with students who may need a little extra attention or may be struggling.

◆ **Sit in on professional development sessions.** Show your staff that PD is important and that you're part of the team and willing to grow and learn as well.

Sometimes, just the simple fact that an administrator makes the effort to be present throughout the building can be enough to proactively prevent issues before they have a chance to occur. Be visible in hallways/classes more than in the office. And don't let your only visits be when you do evaluations. Make them regular so they see you're invested in the learning process. Do them in specials classes too! When your staff see that you are visible, present, and ready to serve, it is a major morale booster for them!

39

Start Each Day
with Reflection

The most successful people I have interviewed over the years start their day with quiet time or a reflection of gratitude. This can be done upon rising early each morning, before the rush of the day begins as we get ready and then sit in rush hour traffic to get to school. I always preferred, as a teacher, to get to school a few minutes early and use the time then to focus and prepare for the day. I would leave home 20 minutes early and use that time in my classroom before students arrived as my quiet time. This worked well because I was on time and didn't need to worry about running in late, and secondly, I needed to destress from the drive into work.

I also did this as an administrator. There was something calming about getting to my office early and just focusing on the tasks of the day. I could check my schedule, emails, and set a goal or two for the day.

What is the purpose of using this time to reflect on the day? To focus and prepare for the day. A great way to start this part of the day is to focus on gratitude. What are you grateful for in your life? Your family, job, friends, and even your health? **Starting the day with gratitude is like filling up your tank for the day! It will be the fuel to get you through the roughest of days.**

Next focus on something you accomplished yesterday. Remember that momentum is important in life, so reflecting

DOI: 10.4324/9781003308218-39

on a success from the day before will put you in the mindset of success and help you focus on being successful today as well. Small successes, especially in education, are a great motivator, even for a veteran educator.

Finally, focus on your goals for the day. It is hard to know if you had a successful day if you don't have measurable goals. These don't have to be big goals, but I have found when I was able to achieve even small goals in a day, I felt much more successful and yes even grateful. Remember you may have a tough job, but it is also a very important and fulfilling job. And one of the ways to prevent burnout is to reflect on the day and prepare for it with a positive mindset.

40

Value and Add Value

If there is one thing we all have in common as humans, it is that we like to be recognized for a job well done. There is not much that makes your day more than when someone acknowledges your hard work, commitment, or going the extra mile for the staff, students, or school. And that just motivates us to want to do more! Well, teachers are no different. Teachers want to work hard for you. When you acknowledge their hard work, show you value them as humans, and even celebrate their work, there is not much they won't do for you as a leader. I truly believe that effective leaders understand that they should not only value their staff, but also *add* value to their staff. The word "appreciate" literally means to add value. So, appreciating teachers and staff adds value to them as individuals and as a team.

And while we are on the topic of value, do you know what teachers value most about administrators? They value leaders who are trusting, supporting, caring, and personable. The irony of this list is that these are the attributes used by administrators to show appreciation for their staff.

Appreciation is not just a pat on the back, but an ability to understand the worth, quality, or importance of something. So, value recognition as a frequent and ongoing activity that builds a strong, positive school culture. See recognition as a necessary ingredient and key driver of school success. Appreciation is shown through building a relationship based on trust, respect, and open communication. Think about it – if you appreciate

DOI: 10.4324/9781003308218-40

someone in your personal life, such as a spouse, you don't just show it once. You show it consistently. You let them know on a continual basis that they are important to you. The same is true of appreciating your students, teachers/staff, and even other administrators. Remember everyone likes to be recognized for hard work, and education in particular is an affirmational profession by nature. So let your teachers and staff know how much you appreciate them and do all you can do help them be their best. It will actually make your job easier.

41

Are You Asking the Right Question?

The best leaders know that in order to truly be effective and successful, you must do one thing really, really well: Ask good questions. And it doesn't stop there. You must not only be asking great, thought-provoking questions, but listening. Asking questions of your staff is a great way to show them you value their opinion and expertise, such as asking them their input on curriculum or textbooks.

But the two most important questions that you can ask are: "How are you doing?" and "How can I help you?" These two questions show that you care about them not just as teachers, but as humans as well. The key is that when you ask these questions, then you have to listen, really listen, to the answers. **If you aren't listening to the ideas and needs of your staff, how can you possibly serve them?**

"How are you doing?" may seem like a simple question, but asking it at the right time can make a big difference. Caring for those you lead is a trademark of a servant leader. Pay attention to your staff and look for signs that they may be struggling. Did you know our faces are the best places in which to read our emotions? It's a window to how we're really feeling. Learning to recognize those micro-expressions of feeling allows us to connect more fully with others. Respectfully recognizing another's emotional state will allow you to know when to ask them how they are doing.

DOI: 10.4324/9781003308218-41

Now most of us have been conditioned to ask that question without really expecting more than the obligatory response of, "I am fine." In fact, it has become so desensitized that no one really listens to the reply. So, you may have to take it a step further to recondition your staff that you really want to know the answer. You may have to start by asking questions like, "How is everything with your family?" Moving the conversation away from the classroom and making it more personal may catch their attention. Even if it takes a little time to get them to open up, don't give up.

When you have built good relationships with your staff, you can tell when someone is having an off day. If you have a teacher who is always smiling, outgoing, and happy, but all of a sudden they seem worried, preoccupied, or stressed out, make sure to check on them. Some staff members may not want to share issues, but when you ask sincerely, they may open up to you. There may be an illness in the family, or they may even be struggling with a health issue. And not that you need all the details, but knowing there is an issue provides you the ability to help out if possible. Do they need a class covered to take a child to the doctor, or maybe need to come in later for a few days because of a family emergency. Never be afraid to ask how someone is doing; make sure you listen, and then take action if needed.

That leads us into the other important question, "How can I help you?" Nothing reflects servant leadership more than "How can I help you," or "How can I serve you?" This question is an expression of humility and support. It should almost be the ending to all your interactions with your staff. I think leaders who pose this question have an understanding of the power of service.

As a leader, it is important to have a pulse on the morale, stress level, and environmental conditions of your teachers, so you can calm high stress situations, or inspire when spirits are waning. You need to especially be mindful of their full plates and recognize key stress time. Don't overload teachers with professional development during report card season. Don't expect committee work or other duties during conference time. Avoid new initiatives and stresses during the end of the term, report-writing periods, or while teachers are grading exams. If there's any way you can lend a hand during these times, whether it's taking on some of the work yourself, or covering a teacher's lunch supervision shift, help shoulder the load for your team.

However, when you ask the question, "How can I help you?" listen, and then be ready to roll up your sleeves and go to work. I know that I personally have rolled up my sleeves many times and jumped into the trenches. I have helped cover classes when a teacher needed to leave early, helped clean up the cafeteria when they were short staffed, and I have helped move more classrooms than I care to remember. Some of these teachers never let go of anything! But when your staff sees that you are sincere and truly there to serve them, then you have captured their heart. Ask the right questions, really listen, and then respond. You will have a staff willing to go to battle with you.

42

Leadership Is All About Relationships

While we all may dream of days, or maybe even weeks, where we could just be alone, the reality is that every aspect of our lives is based upon relationships. Whether it is with a spouse, family, friends, colleagues, or even students, everything is based upon relationships.

Since so much of our existence is based upon these relationships, it is important to make sure we have healthy ones. I like to joke that I had a former principal who said we were going to be like family. But what he didn't tell us was that it was a dysfunctional family! Now you may have experienced a similar situation as a teacher or even as an administrator.

I get countless messages and emails from teachers all around the world who wish their administrators spent more time developing positive relationships with the staff. I think part of the disconnect is that people are often promoted to leadership roles based upon past competencies. I think, for the most part, IQ also plays a role in being promoted. However, as I have shared for many years, it is our EQ (emotional intelligence) that best translates to success as a leader. As a teacher, you may not have needed that type of interaction and affirmation from your administration. However, most teachers do need that affirmation – and, well, most people do like to be noticed and appreciated for the work they do. And don't forget the story of captain Mike

DOI: 10.4324/9781003308218-42

Abrashoff that I shared earlier. It wasn't the IQ of the ship captain but his ability to connect with the crew that made the biggest difference.

Most relationships are formed based upon a level of respect or love, and every healthy relationship needs trust. **Whether it is with your students, staff, or administrator colleagues, make sure you create relationships based upon respect and trust.** If you think about it, during the school year you may spend as much of your waking hours at school as you do at home. So, don't underestimate the importance of building those relationships. It is similar to the time a coach spends with athletes. I often use a picture of a young Kareem Abdul Jabbar at UCLA with his coach John Wooden juxtaposed to a picture of them decades later when they are much older, with Jabbar holding onto an aging Wooden as they walk onto a basketball court. It is a powerful example of how important relationships are to the learning/coaching process and that relationships can impact the rest of our lives.

Finally, I remember my own principal from high school. His name was Mr. Kent. He would always greet people, seemed to know everyone, and showed he cared. Even though I was just a high school student, I picked up on the importance of developing relationships with those you lead from him. I tried to emulate that when I became I an administrator myself.

So, focus on those relationships, and see what a difference it makes in your staff and the culture of your school.

43

Foster Emotional Connectedness

A leader's ability to engage people at the emotional level has emerged as the strongest indicator of leadership potential and performance. In fact, emotional intelligence (EQ) is a key hallmark of great leaders. So, to be a successful principal, your EQ may be the most important area of influence you have. Fortunately, if you don't have the highest EQ, it is something that can be developed; it will just require a little focus. With increased EQ, you have the ability to connect better with your staff, which I call Emotional Connectedness.

Think back to your favorite leader. Was it someone who was great at budgets, or did you say, "Wow, this principal really knows how to create a schedule!" Probably not. In fact, it probably wasn't the management skills of the administrator that inspired you. It was likely something intangible, such as how the administrator left people feeling motivated, inspired, and even appreciated. These high EQ principals ask teachers things like, "How are you doing? How is the family? How can I help you?" They seek to connect with their staff on a personal level.

Some people are simply not good at the emotional aspect of leadership, and these are also the people who tend to struggle in getting their staff committed to their leadership. It's important to remember that when dealing with humans, we aren't dealing with creatures of logic, but rather creatures of emotions. **In fact,**

DOI: 10.4324/9781003308218-43

most of the decisions we make are based on emotions. We try to justify our actions to others or to ourselves with logic, but emotions are the catalyst to our decisions and actions. How you display your emotions and how you connect with your staff's emotions will be the difference between success and failure. Remember when you make the emotional connections, you capture their heart, because that is what will create a committed staff.

When it comes to emotional intelligence, you have to first control your own emotions. To be respected, principals cannot keep people guessing about how they will react to a particular situation. Principals who demonstrate erratic dispositions don't last long in the job. So, learning to control your emotions is the first step to building strong positive relationships with your staff. In fact, **until you learn to lead from within, you cannot lead others.** While there are several factors in building high EQ, these four will accelerate your relationship connections most effectively:

- ◆ **Self-awareness** is the ability to recognize your emotions and the effects of your moods on other people. The ability to recognize an emotion as it "happens" is the key to your EQ. If you evaluate your emotions, you can manage them. The major elements of self-awareness are emotional awareness and self-confidence. The place that leaders struggle the most is in self-awareness – understanding how people see them and what they really look like from the outside. We need to be self-aware. When you discover what you need to be doing differently, what you're poor at, that's what opens the door to improved performance. That's because it allows you to put people in places of strengths where you may not be strong. So, self-awareness is key.
- ◆ **Self-regulation** is the ability to manage disruptive emotions and impulses (fear, anxiety, anger, sadness); thinking before you act; and taking responsibility for your actions. You often have little control over when you experience emotions. You can, however, have some say in how long an emotion will last by using a number of

techniques to alleviate negative emotions such as anger, anxiety, or depression. A few of these techniques include recasting a situation in a more positive light, or taking a long walk and meditation or prayer. Self-regulation involves traits such as self-control, trustworthiness, conscientiousness, and adaptability.

◆ **Empathy** is the ability to sense others' perceptions and feelings; seeing what others need to bolster their ability; and listening to and validating the concerns of others. The more skilled you are at discerning the feelings behind others' actions or reactions, the better you can control your reactions to them. An empathetic person excels at service orientation, developing others, and understanding others.

◆ **Relationship intelligence** is the ability to understand the emotional fibers that make up others and to treat them accordingly; the ability to persuade, initiate change, and create group synergy. The development of good interpersonal skills is paramount to success in your life and career. In today's always-connected world, everyone has immediate access to technical knowledge. Thus, "people skills" are even more important now because you must possess a high EQ to better understand, empathize, and negotiate with others in a global economy. Among the most useful skills are influence, communication, conflict management, and building rapport.

This isn't to say that you need to be an overly emotional person to be a good leader. In fact, wearing your emotions on your sleeve means that you probably don't have a high EQ. So, it's really more about managing emotions and understanding how to engage the emotions of those you lead to maximize results and commitment. I believe that to be an effective leader, you have to learn to be emotionally connected rather than emotionally distant. You should be someone to whom people naturally gravitate. These are upbeat individuals who exude a positive vibe. Being emotionally connected creates a culture where your staff will want to give their best.

44

Find Yourself a Good Mentor

Moving from an assistant principal position to a principal position is much like moving from a student teacher position into the role of lead teacher. Yes, you have experience, but when you hold the keys to the kingdom, it becomes a very different ball game. Even an experienced principal moving into a new school may experience new challenges and issues that they haven't encountered before and may have them looking for a mentor or at least a confidante with whom they can confide and bounce ideas.

The reality is that in the past principals were often thrown into the job with a sink or swim approach from the district level. This may be because they were treated the same way when they first became principals themselves. However, with the high turnover rate and burnout rate of educational leaders, many districts have put formal mentoring programs into place. I know of several systems that have yearlong mentoring groups for new leaders in various roles, such as for APs and for principals. These "cohorts" meet regularly, focus on topics such as leadership strengths, where they take tests like strengths finders, and they read and discuss leadership books.

Since leaving the K–12 setting to teach leadership at the graduate level, as well as speak and write on leadership, I have had the opportunity to connect with many leaders not just in education, but in other fields as well. I truly believe that good leadership is good leadership regardless of the field. But one of

DOI: 10.4324/9781003308218-44

the things that drives effective leadership is good mentoring. Everyone is born with certain talents and strengths that can help them be more effective leaders, but never underestimate the importance of a quality mentor or mentors. I have several leaders that I mentor on a formal and informal basis. I usually meet with these individuals once a month for coffee and conversation. With those I mentor, we usually read a book and discuss topics like building relationships and empowering and developing followers into leaders. I enjoy books like *It's Your Ship* by Mike Abrashoff, which is about his experience leading the *USS Benfold*. It has great stories, but it has many great leadership tips and advice as well. Reading is an amazing mentoring tool all by itself. In fact, did you know the average CEO reads 60 books a year? They know the importance of not just getting to the top of the ladder, but staying on top of latest research, trends, ideas, etc. to remain on top.

If your district has a mentoring program, take full advantage of it. However, there is also nothing wrong with having a mentor or friend in another school that you can turn to if needed, or you may even be able to connect with someone on social media. Since great leadership is not confined to a certain field, find someone you trust, even if they aren't in education. **Although you might believe that your experiences are unique, you will find that others have experienced many of the same things, even the things that feel most personal to you.** This also helps you know you're not alone or experiencing something unique. Choose an experienced principal as a mentor, someone who will listen, advise, and catch you before you jump off the proverbial cliff. Finally, a new principal, in fact every principal, needs a trusted colleague, friend, mentor, or confidante who can provide sage advice, listen to occasional venting, offer unwavering support, and, most important, bring laughter to the situation. All principals need someone supportive they can count on for difficult days. For that level of support, there is no substitute.

45

Stay Young at Heart

Nearly half of school level administrators report feeling burned out. While working in education can be rewarding, it can also be hard work. So, one of the most important qualities of an administrator is to stay young at heart. Once you stop enjoying time with the kids, teachers, and staff, once you stop laughing often and enjoying the little things, then you will lose the joy of your job.

I love when I hear administrators who have been in education for 15, 20, or even 25 years say that they couldn't imagine doing anything else. These are the administrators who are still young at heart. I have been fortunate to travel all around the world, and I can say with confidence that the best administrators are those who still get excited about school, about making a difference in the lives of students and staff.

I remember a professor I had in graduate school – her name was Dr. Mosely. She was big into fitness and while she was in her 60s, you would have thought she was in her 20s. She was fit, full of life, and just seemed to live in the moment. I remember her telling me once that I was young at heart and that she hoped I would never change. Now, she might have been trying to tell me that I was just immature for my age, but I took it as a compliment because I knew she was young at heart, and I sure didn't mind being compared to her and the energy she brought to even a graduate program!

Staying young at heart is a mindset more than anything else. I have met many veteran educators who seem to be ageless

DOI: 10.4324/9781003308218-45

in their passion, joy, and excitement for learning. They all bring a high energy vibe to the school culture. Afterall, since we are dealing with students, shouldn't that be the kind of energy we want to bring?

I have often said that within reason, a school should sound more like a construction site than a museum. This means there is high energy, it can get a little noisy at times, and there are a lot of things going on throughout the building. Don't be afraid of a little controlled chaos, because that is how students engage, interact, and yes even learn.

So, if you are like me in my 50s, or maybe younger, and you feel like you need an energy boost for school, here are a few tips to help you keep that mindset.

1. **Exercise your body and mind daily.** If you want to keep your body strong, spry, and flexible, you need to be active.
2. **Make sure to get adequate sleep.**
3. **Share a hobby with staff or students.** Or better yet help a teacher with an outside the box project they are going to try.
4. **Be an active school community member.**
5. **Embrace new technology and entertainment.**
6. **Have fun!**

Being a school leader is a tough job and a high stress job. It is easy to burn out, just like teachers do. So be mindful of self-care and incorporate those tips into your daily routine, so you can create high energy within your school.

46

Follow Your Path

Now this quote is a great piece of advice whether in your career or in your personal life. As an administrator, we often feel pressure to act or even lead a certain way. You may find yourself trying to be like another administrator, or like some model of leadership created by the district. But the reality is you are an amazing administrator in your own right, or you at least have the potential within you to be. The key is to use your talents and follow your heart as you hone your skills as an administrator. The same can be said in your personal life, where people have certain expectations of you or you feel like you have expectations that you have placed on yourself.

I felt this way early in life, but in my 20s, my father shared a piece of advice that I never forgot and it's the premise of this quote. I shared it earlier in this book, but I think it's an important reminder here, too. He said, "Son, follow your path. Don't worry what others say you should do or what path you think is expected of you, but follow your path." My father may not have known just how impactful that piece of advice was to me. Then again, he may have known it was exactly the words that I needed to hear. Either way, I am so thankful that I listened.

This doesn't mean that your path will be easy, or that you will always get to go in the direction you think. **But it is important to stay true to what you believe is best for you.** I can admit that I had doors that didn't open for me that I was certain should have been open. There were times when I might have been overlooked

DOI: 10.4324/9781003308218-46

for a position that I knew I was qualified for, but I didn't let that keep me down or defeated. I simply reflected, adjusted if needed, and kept moving forward.

As a teacher, administrator, professor, and now as a speaker, I have always followed my own path. I felt pressured by others at times to take a certain position or not to take a certain risk, but I stayed true to my path. I have experienced failures, but I have always believed in myself and my purpose. As I travel the world now, inspiring and affirming teachers and administrators of their great work, I can say that I would not have changed one thing! So, don't feel like you have to live up to others' expectations, or do things like someone else. Whether you are content where you are or think there is more out there, just follow your path and trust me you will be glad you did!

47

Be Approachable

If there is one attribute that is critical for the success of a leader, it is being approachable.

This is especially important when you're the principal, since we know educators tend to be highly agreeable and don't like conflict. The more comfortable they feel with you and the more accessible they think you are, then the better your relationship with them will become. If you isolate yourself, or feel you need to distance yourself from the others, it might only serve to alienate you and put you in a position where you're viewed with distrust or even resentment. This doesn't mean you're trying to be their buddy, because they want a leader, not another friend, but it doesn't mean that you shouldn't be friendly.

Approachability is having other people feel comfortable bringing either good news or bad news to you, and knowing their leader will listen to them. So, go out of your way to have personal exchanges with your employees and co-workers. You don't need to build friendships, but there's no reason why you can't get to know each other.

Personal working relationships are important for cultivating a sense of team, and if people see you as another person on the team, they'll be more receptive when you disclose your ideas or opinions. The key here is to seem imperfect, approachable, and human. Some of the ways I kept that approachable side was to always inquire about events in my teachers' lives. If a child or family member was sick or maybe someone was graduating or

DOI: 10.4324/9781003308218-47

getting married, I would ask about them. Teachers appreciate it when you treat them as humans with lives outside of school, and not just the teacher in the classroom.

Being approachable also involves your verbal and even non-verbal cues. When I mentor leaders now, I like to share the phrase from the old television program *Fantasy Island*. When the plane would land on the island, the host, Mr. Roake would be there with the staff to greet the new guests, and he would always say, "Smiles everyone, smiles!" Let that be your motto as well.

In fact, did you know a smile makes you look more attractive and approachable?

One of the most common responses when I talk to teachers about approachability of their administrators is that they always have a serious look on their face and act like they are always running late somewhere. They often don't even say hello in the hallway. Regardless of how busy you are, always take time to smile, say hello, and be approachable. Here are seven points to keep in mind. Watch the difference they make with your staff.

1. **Don't pretend to know it all.** They know you don't, so this mindset makes you appear disingenuous and unapproachable.
2. **Share stories to connect.** It can be a story of struggle, failure, or triumph. Just connect.
3. **Admit when you're wrong.** Nothing is more authentic than a person in a position of power admitting they did something wrong. Make mistakes, just not excuses.
4. **Remember what it was like as a teacher and how your experiences may help them.** And remember to jump in the trenches with them as much as possible.
5. **Have a sense of humor.** You work in a building full of students, so smiling and laughing are a prerequisite. Smiles everyone, smiles!
6. **Take time to ask staff about life events.**
7. **Never be so rushed that you don't make eye contact in the halls or greet staff and students as you pass them.**

48

Find Your Voice

Did you know education is probably the main profession where people tend to be most agreeable? Highly agreeable people are great for encouraging, supporting, affirming, and many of the traits we desire in educators. However, some of the negatives of being highly agreeable are that we don't like conflict, aren't good at negotiating, and rarely speak up for ourselves.

Since most administrators were once teachers, this means many of you share these traits as well. Once you realize the importance of leading and not just managing, you can develop your own voice. **Voice is your overall expression of who you are ... to yourself, your community, and to the world.** This voice will allow you to communicate your needs and wants while contributing your talents and capabilities. Your expression is the culmination of finding, creating, and using your voice to make a difference for yourself and your life. Discovering your values, creating outcomes, sharing your influence, developing courage, and conveying your overall expression are all ingredients for finding and using your *voice* as a leader. In our schools, there are numerous opportunities to become leaders. Besides the typical administration roles, teachers can have leadership roles such as grade-level chairs, department chairs, and instructional coaches. The guidance counselors and support staff also have leadership roles.

All of these leadership positions will not only have different roles and responsibilities, but will also have different

DOI: 10.4324/9781003308218-48

personalities, which means they all need to find their own voice that will not only help each individual succeed, but be able to successfully work together, too. As I have often said, focusing on your strengths and developing the strengths of those you lead will make you and your staff more successful. So, part of finding your voice has already been accomplished by understanding your talents and strengths. For example, some people may not feel like they are a leader or possess the skills to lead, so they never find their voice as a leader.

However, understanding that you possess talents and strengths to lead should give you the confidence to speak up. Don't let fear or defeating self-talk, like, "I am a new administrator," or "There are others who know much more than I do" keep you from finding your voice. Also, don't let others drown out your voice with negativity, especially your inner voice. In fact, when you have the courage to speak up, even to those who lead you, you may inspire others to find their voice as well. You need and deserve to be heard; you are a leader after all!

49

Enjoy the Joy of Education

Every aspect of education has always been a point of joy for me. As a teacher, I loved to watch students come to school with excitement and anticipation of a new year, new friends, and new adventures. As an administrator, I loved to watch teachers enter the new year with excitement and anticipation too!

In fact, education should be about the joy of new adventures, the joy of building relationships, and the joy of learning. Sometimes I feel like standardized testing and unrealistic expectations placed on students and on teachers have stolen away that joy.

Don't lose that joy of serving in the noblest of professions. I admit that at times it can be easy to feel defeated, joyless, and unsatisfied, but even if you aren't in the ideal school setting or supported as much as you could be from the district, just focus on the things in your life that are great. I have walked in schools where it seems the energy is zapped out of me as I enter the door, and I ask myself who stole their joy? Who or what is keeping this administration and staff from enjoying their job? Then I walk in schools where the energy is electric! Where everyone has a smile and is engaging. This is almost always due to the administrators who work to make the learning environment fun and engaging. Yes, education is a serious business, but when you work with students, there has to be a balance of fun and joy to the learning. And trust me, students pick up on the vibes of the administration and staff and it affects how they engage as well.

DOI: 10.4324/9781003308218-49

So how can you create a climate of joy in the school? First of all, be visible. It makes a big difference, much like it does with teachers who are in the hallways or greeting students at the door. When you are in the halls, classrooms, cafeteria, bus, or car lines, you create connections. In fact, how you interact in those areas is more important than how you interact in a meeting. And have fun. It has been said that children laugh 300 to 400 times a day and that adults laugh around 30 times a day. But I know adults who laugh maybe once a week! So, help create a climate where everyone enjoys being at school.

Finally, never miss a chance to give shoutouts to your amazing staff. I was at a school in Las Vegas where the principal started back to school by having staff "walk the red carpet"! He not only found ways to create a fun and engaging environment, but he also designed the teachers' lounge around massage chairs! He kept snacks and treats in there and encouraged teachers to take advantage of it. Trust me when I say, these teachers enjoyed coming to work every day! Here's the best part of this: When your staff enjoys being there, it makes you enjoy being there too!

50

Never Underestimate Your Legacy

Never underestimate the importance of your role as a leader or the legacy that you leave behind. I can still remember my principal from first grade! And yes, that was almost half a century ago! But I still remember how he encouraged us to be our best and had special treats for the students based upon good behavior or making good grades. I especially remember that he took us to McDonalds if we made all A's on our report cards. My family rarely ate out back then, which probably most families didn't, so it was a special treat for me. It made me think of him as someone who was on our side as students and not just the person to go to when in trouble. All these years later, I still remember the impact he had on us.

And then there was my cousin Tammy, who was a teacher for over 25 years. She taught special education, and later she was an administrator for new teacher induction and special education. Regardless of the class or grade level, one thing was always true, she loved her students, and they loved her. Whether it was a hug or school supplies, she always had what the students needed. **She always made sure students were having a good day, even if only while in her class.**

Sadly, Tammy passed away a couple of years ago from cancer, but that was not the end of her story. Her last request, when she was faced with her own mortality, was for friends and family to

DOI: 10.4324/9781003308218-50

bring backpacks full of supplies to her funeral instead of flowers. She was always thinking of others first and said there were many students in need within the community.

At the funeral, there were over 100 backpacks lined along the chapel pews and upfront. About 50 teachers were honorary pallbearers and after the service, they formed a long line for the casket to be carried through to the hearse. I actually posted a picture of the backpacks sitting by the pews in an empty chapel on Twitter and it went viral, reaching millions of people worldwide! Every major media outlet in the world ran a story on what they called the teacher's last request, backpacks in lieu of flowers. It was one of those feel-good stories that resonated with everyone, not just teachers.

A teacher who lived in relative anonymity for her whole life became a source of inspiration for the world with her final lesson, which was to put others first. Countless students she had taught through the years spoke of the positive impact she had on them and how she changed their lives. Several teachers shared the influence she had on them and wished they could tell her the impact she had on their life. People from all around the world sent backpacks to her school district because they felt such a connection to her teacher heart.

So, on those tough days, remember, you aren't just making a difference, but you are planting seeds that will sprout in the lives of students and your staff. You are creating a legacy that will live on through them long after your journey is completed.

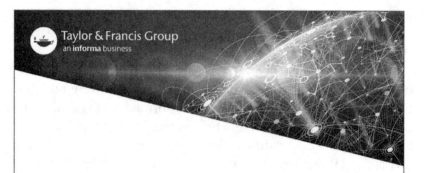

Printed in the United States
by Baker & Taylor Publisher Services